DON'T BE
BETTER
BE
BEST

STEPHEN M. LAW

TWO PENNY
—— PUBLISHING ——

To my Heavenly Father,

If not for Your protection and guidance in my life, this book would never have come to be. It's the words You give me that I want to share with the world!

To my wife,

If not for your love and support, I would not have finished this book. At least, it would definitely have a lot more errors without your gentle yet persistent grammatical guidance!

To my son,

I haven't met you yet, but more than holding this book in my hands, I can't wait to hold you. I hope that as you grow, you will indeed be best and change this world. I wrote this book in the hopes to help improve the world you are coming into. I love you, and I always will!

TABLE OF CONTENTS

WHY BETTER IS NOT ENOUGH

BE BETTER, OR BE BEST?

Good, better, best. Never let it rest.
'Til your good is better,
and your better is best.

–*St. Jerome*

We hear it all the time: "become better," "be a better you," etc... but isn't it about time we became MORE than just "better"?

It's true, we want to be better, but the word "better" itself can be limiting. Saying "I'm working on becoming better" is much like when someone says "I'll do it later," but later can mean *in a minute* or *in a year*.

Here is an example: Someone could say one day, "I want to have better health," and then the next day, "I only eat fast food twice a day instead of three times a day." Yes, it's better, but it's far from best. People often find themselves checking off the "becoming better" box, but then they stop there. What if our goal wasn't just to be better, but to become best? I'm not saying we need to be the best at everything, but rather, understand how to give our best.

Giving your best will not result in just being better.

Your best won't settle for better. Your best wants more; it wants to go beyond better. Your best is what can push and motivate you to actually **be best**.

But how can we pull out our best? How can we push past our limits to do more than we think we can? In this book, I hope to demonstrate and guide what it looks like to be a "Best-Giver."

THE MAKING OF A BEST-GIVER

> *If you only do what you can do,*
> *you will never be more*
> *than who you are.*
> –Master Shifu, Kung Fu Panda 3

I have always had a spirit of competitiveness. I remember competitions on the playground to see who could count to 100 the fastest, or who got the best grades on class projects. That continued as I grew older, and while I tried to come out on top, that was not always the case. At first I just wanted to get ahead, but over time I realized getting first place or being "number one" didn't mean very much to me. What mattered more to me was to see myself improving with each effort. Instead of being focused on getting better results than others, my competitiveness soon turned inward. I enjoyed finding people who were ahead of me because they showed me that I had more work to do. My goal became to push past the limits that surrounded me. I didn't let any external circumstance keep me from that goal.

I realized my desire to go beyond expectations around the time *The Matrix* trilogy was popular. This dystopian world fascinated me, and the idea of someone potentially breaking the mold that society had constructed was intriguing. I wanted that "power," but didn't know how to get it. I began asking myself, "Is it possible to do better? To be more? What is my actual best? What is the limit, and can I move past it?"

> *I enjoyed finding people who were ahead of me because they showed me that I had more work to do.*

In the episode "World Record" from the animated *Matrix* series, a runner named Dan is dissatisfied with his current race time and believes that he can become faster. He refused to accept that there was a limit to how fast he could run, and throughout the episode, he kept pushing himself to be faster. At the climax of the incident, he defied expectations and ran quickly enough to launch himself "out of the Matrix." He then found there was much more to reality than he had been taught.

I was aware that we do not live in a Matrix, but this cartoon episode made me wonder if I could also push myself to be more. I questioned what the limits of reality were. I wondered what it would look like if I continually pushed myself to reach beyond those limits and be intentional about giving my best. I wanted to be a "Best-Giver."

I have heard stories about people who have done precisely that: stories of people like Roger Bannister, who was the first man to surpass the four-minute mile in 1954. No one thought it was possible, which drove him to push past his limits. There are prodigies like Ludwig van Beethoven who published his first work, 9 Variations in C Minor, at the age of 12, and continued to become one of the greatest musical geniuses of all time! Another example is the inspiring artist Ann Adams, who contracted polio. She became incapable of breathing on her own and became mostly paralyzed. After learning to draw by holding a pencil with her mouth, she improved enough to fully support herself with just her art! These stories prove that our limits may just be obstacles trying to keep us from making a new reality for ourselves.

The concept of being a Best-Giver began to take shape for the rest of my life. I integrated that mindset into everything I did. In high school, college, work, sports, and games, I always believed there was more I could do if I pushed myself hard and worked smart enough.

Now, I am not saying I am the best at everything I do! I know I am not, and I am thankful that there are always people out there doing something better and inspiring me to push myself further. I will always keep the mindset that if I am going to do something, I will give it everything I have. I want to give my best!

Often, our way of thinking will shape the person we become, the obstacles we overcome, and our achievements.

I have spent the majority of my life serving or involved in church ministry. If there is one major thing I have learned, it is that reality can be more significant than what I *think*. Often, our way of thinking will shape the person we become, the obstacles we overcome, and our achievements. Over the years, I have applied this and seen its fruit. I believe I have some insight that might help you do the same.

I believe that you are capable of incredible success. You can accomplish more than just ordinary results. The fact that you are reading this book is a statement to your desire to do more and be better. There are a plethora of self-help books out there, and I believe you should read or listen to as many of them as you can. Learn from them and find what works for YOU.

That is how I hope to help. I have always been passionate about making this world a better place. While that is a lofty dream, I believe it starts with helping others. If more people drive themselves to improve and strive to succeed, I know it will make the world better. In the following chapters, I hope to help guide you forward through the process of building your best life. I cannot promise you riches and fame, but if you embrace the concepts in this book, you will indeed find a "best" version of yourself!

Keep in mind this does not happen overnight. You will have to start small and take the steps necessary to see the big picture. From there, you will learn how to set up a foundation to learn the truth about your identity. And just like what is right in any other project, you'll need the right materials to move forward. However, even with those materials, you need to find the drive to put it all together. There will be difficult times and trials that may seem to stall your progress, but you can take comfort knowing that you don't have to face them alone. The "Be Best" lifestyle is designed to breed success, joy, and excitement. These things will help you make the most out of life and lead you to leave a legacy that continues to help others follow in your footsteps and, hopefully, surpass them!

Join me as we build the qualities of the Best-Giver. Let's not settle for being better - let's **be best!**

I've always tried to do my best today, think about tomorrow, and maybe dream a bit about the future. But doing your best in the present has to be the rule. You won't become a general unless you become a good first lieutenant.

–General Colin Powell

FINDING YOUR BEST PLAN

THE POWER OF LEARNING

1

The beginning of wisdom is this: Get wisdom.
Though it costs all you have, get understanding.
Proverbs 4:7

Have you ever noticed how, when we are young, we tend to think we have the answers for everything? We run through life without thinking about the pros and cons, or how to be most effective. In our minds, it's no big deal. We can handle it. We have what it takes.

I recently gave a talk about the problem of regret. Regret is something nobody wants to have to deal with, but unfortunately, we seem to face it far too often.

New Oxford Dictionary defines regret as "the feeling of sadness, repentance, or disappointment, over something happened or that has been done, especially in regards to missing an opportunity."

I discussed how to avoid regret, and the answer seemed so simple—know the future. If you know the future, you don't have to regret your choices because you already know what the outcome will be. No one purposely makes a choice knowing it will lead them to regret later.

Of course, there's a problem with this answer. How can we possibly know the future? How do we know what is going to work, and what is not? Well, we can't with 100% accuracy, but we can think ahead and brainstorm results.

An example of this can be seen in a story often

referenced from the Bible, found in Matthew 7:24-27.

Everyone who hears these words of mine and puts them into practice is like a wise man who built his house on the rock. The rain came down, the streams rose, and the winds blew and beat against that house, yet it did not fall, because it had its foundation on the rock. But everyone who hears these words of mine and does not put them into practice is like a foolish man who built his house on sand. The rain came down, the streams rose, and the winds blew and beat against that house, and it fell with a great crash.

This simple story has deep meaning. If we want something to last, we need to think ahead. If we plan for possible adversity, we won't have regrets when it arrives. It goes along with the saying "It's better to have something and not need it than to need it and not have it." Ask yourself, "What do I need to have in my plan now so I don't have regrets later?"

No matter how beautiful your house is, if you don't plan for trouble, it is at risk of ruin! In the story of the two builders, the first person immediately reacted based on what they saw, not what could have been. The second person, on the other hand, thought through the long term sustainability of his product. This scenario is not just about foundation choice. It's also about thinking through possibilities, having wisdom, and seeking guidance so you can create a blueprint for success.

HOW TO FORM A BLUEPRINT

No one wants to go through life without a plan. But how often do we find ourselves saying "hindsight is 20/20"? We want to make the best decision, but we mess up. We wish we had done things differently. I'm sure at some point you have said, "If I had known..." "If I could do it again, I would..." "Now, I know for next time..."

Maybe it hurts to hear that because you've been there. We've all had moments where regret sinks in. In those moments, we are forced to decide if we should keep going and if the goal is worth it. A blueprint can prevent those

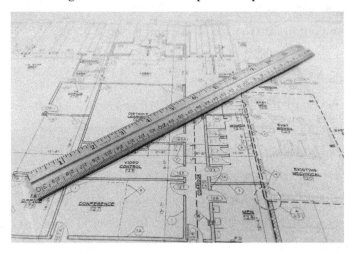

moments from happening. So let's talk about how to make a blueprint for success without regret.

> *Wisdom is necessary for creating the best blueprint of your life.*

If you have ever looked at a blueprint before, you know there are a lot of details. At first glance, it can seem overwhelming: lines going every which way, numbers scattered all over, shapes and symbols that seem complicated and make the plan hard to interpret. Without it, though, we find ourselves destined for failure—or, with lots of future projects to fix the things we overlooked.

In the following chapters, we will discuss the various parts necessary to build the best success. Let's start with putting together our blueprint, the "BEST plan." Unless you are in architecture, you're going to need some help putting this together. Architects would not just pick up a blue sheet of paper and start drawing without knowing the plan. Before they begin crafting the blueprint, they start brainstorming and sketching out the concept of their goal. This leads to understanding what is needed so they can craft the blueprint necessary for success. That understanding is wisdom.

Wisdom is necessary for creating the best blueprint

of your life. You can choose just to start throwing 2 x 4's and concrete together and see what happens, or you can think through what you want and need to plan out how to succeed. But what does wisdom look like? Where does it come from? Life should be a constant pursuit of wisdom, but knowing where to find it will make the experience a lot more enjoyable!

Keep in mind that education does not necessarily equal success, and a lack of education does not necessarily mean a lack of success. There are plenty of people who have done incredible things without the "expected prerequisite" education or even without a college diploma!

- In 1855, John D. Rockefeller left high school to start working. Within ten years, he launched his refining business that led to his future wealth.
- In 1903, Henry Ford founded the Ford Motor Company, despite having almost no "formal" education.
- In 1972, at the age of 17, Steve Jobs started college just to drop out and start chasing new ideas and dreams, leading him to start Apple Computer Inc. in 1976.

These men all achieved a historic success, even while lacking a proper form of education. That is to say, education does not guarantee wisdom, nor is education the only path to wisdom. Instead, they sought after their dreams, learning through experience and from the knowledge of who they surrounded themselves with. The choice to skip formal education and chase dreams has not worked for everyone. There are far more disappointing realities where people barely make ends meet while chasing a dream. I hope they find success, but while progress is possible without furthering your education, your chances of success can be improved if you do work toward a degree. Regardless of which path you choose, remember, success is not dependent on one's education, but a willingness to learn.

Success is not dependent on one's education, but a willingness to learn.

I was always at church throughout my childhood and teen years, mostly because my parents worked there as the children's pastors. I learned quickly there were some stereotypes about pastor's kids. There was an expectation that eventually, they would grow up

Will you choose to learn from other's experiences or your own?

to be troublemakers. I had to choose if I would let others' expectations define me or prove them wrong. I knew some of those kids who indeed became the stereotype. I had heard the stories, which meant I knew what NOT to do. I decided to learn from others instead of learning from my own mistakes.

It's true: many say experience is the best teacher, and there are lots of people who have experienced incredible things, both positive and negative. The question is, will you choose to learn from other's experiences or your own?

> *It's said that a wise person learns*
> *from his mistakes.*
> *A wiser one learns from others' mistakes.*
> *But the wisest person of all learns*
> *from others' successes.*
> *–John C. Maxwell*

GUIDANCE AND THE POWER OF LEARNING

We all want a good outcome. We hope to find success, and typically, we want it to come quickly. That's why we look for books like this one to help us find the most efficient way to succeed. We try to do it ourselves, but it's not so easy. So we seek advice and wisdom from someone who's been there. We look for someone who has already achieved success. Before you start making your blueprint, it might be worth finding a guide to lead you in the right direction.

When I was in high school, my friends and I enjoyed extreme sports. We started with skateboarding. A few of my friends were rather talented, but I was never very good at it. I loved the feeling of rushing forward at high speeds and even catching some air time, but I always struggled to keep the board with me in the air. One day, while on a church youth ski trip, we learned about a new sport. We saw a London-based documentary that was being aired in America for the first time. This documentary introduced the sport of parkour and free-running to America. In my high school mind, it was everything I enjoyed about skateboarding without the board. I could fly through the air and only have to focus on my own two feet. (If you're not sure what parkour is, do a quick Google search to see countless videos now.)

We immediately started training. The problem was, it was new. There were not any video tutorials made yet. There were no "professional trainers" or classes to take. All we could find were some snapshots or illustrations from a few scarce videos. So we took it upon ourselves to learn all we could through our own experience.

We pulled out a few cheap mats that our church had for the elementary students and started to learn by trial and error. Of course, we wanted to learn how to do the cool-looking flips that we saw on the video, like the "wall-flip." We would run at a wall and kick in the air with all our might. We ended up falling on our backs again, again, and again. At least we compiled some funny videos of us falling to go along with the scrapes and bruises. Some of us learned right away, but others took a bit longer. In my case, the backflip was my problem. I would give it everything I had but continued to fail time and time again. After about a year of trying, I started putting my efforts into other skills. It wasn't until we were taking a capoeira class (a Brazilian martial art that resembles break dancing) that the instructor did a backflip, and it looked perfect! I had found my guide.

Of course, I asked him how he did it so effortlessly. He broke it down for me in a simple way that I had missed from just looking at photos. He used his experience and wisdom to show me what I was doing wrong. That day I learned how to do a backflip, mostly because of the guidance of someone better than me.

Today, the sport of parkour has become widely known thanks to shows like *Ninja Warrior*, and most chase scenes in movies. It is great to see so many people interested in becoming practitioners of the sport. Thanks to the sixteen years of training under my belt, I am now able to teach people in a few hours how to do what took me a year to learn.

There is something to be said about surrounding yourself with wise people who offer guidance. A quote I hear often says "Show me your friends, and I'll show you your future." It's not to say that you will exactly become your friends, but if you are surrounding yourself with "friends" who couldn't care less about improving their life, there is a good chance you'll find yourself feeling the same way. If you surround yourself with forward thinkers, innovators, people who are always giving their best, you'll notice that it drives you forward as well. It's inspiring!

> *If we keep doing the same thing the wrong way, we will not improve.*

People pay countless dollars for mentors, teachers, and tutors to help guide them on how to succeed in each new endeavor. Why? Because we want to do better, but we don't know how. If you can, find the best guide to help you learn how to accomplish your goals. Just remember, paying for that guide does not guarantee success. It still takes effort. If we keep doing the same thing the wrong way, we will not improve. Sure, you may get "better" at doing it that "wrong" way, but that is not the goal. The goal is to do it the best way. If you want to be better, you need to give your best. In every effort, be a **Best-Giver**.

> *How often do you find yourself dwelling on regret instead of looking toward your future?*

BEST PRACTICES

1. How often do you find yourself dwelling on regret instead of looking toward your future?
2. What past experiences have helped shape your story?
3. What method do you have to help track and remember teachable moments?
4. Is there someone or something that you are intentionally learning from?
5. If you don't have a mentor, who is someone you would want guidance from?
6. What is something you want more wisdom in?
7. What steps can you take to achieve that wisdom?

SETTING YOUR BEST FOUNDATION

KNOW YOUR IDENTITY

2

Whatever you are, be a good one.
–William Makepeace Thackeray

Before you start paying for some top-level guide or coach, you need to start with figuring out what you want to learn. You've already started putting your blueprint together. Now we are going to continue to imagine our life like a house that we want to build. It's necessary to learn how to build a house, but a house can mean a lot of different things. Merriam-Webster defines a house as "a building in which something is sheltered or stored." In one area of the world, that might just mean some metal sheeting and foliage, or it could look like a boat, or maybe it's defined by square feet or beds/baths. Some houses have pools and man-caves, and some may have offices and guest bedrooms. If you went to a builder and only said, "Build me a house," the chances of getting what you want would be slim to none. You would have to give a lot more detail. You would have to decide what that house consists of and how it would look. In chapter one, we talked about how seeking wisdom and guidance would shape our blueprint. We also saw that the contents of a house would mean nothing if we didn't adequately plan by setting the right foundation.

Foundation:

foun·da·tion | \ faun-dā-shen

1: a basis (such as a tenet, principle, or axiom) upon which something stands or is supported

2: an underlying base or support

Before we go deep into the contents of our house, we have to start with the foundation. What is the purpose of your house? Will it be big enough to host large parties? Will it be home for many rambunctious children or pets? Will it be in sunny Florida where hurricanes often visit? Before you start the building process, keep all these things in mind to construct the right foundation.

Your foundation will depend on several important factors. Size, strength, layout—a lot goes into planning out a foundation. It will probably look different for everyone based on the specified needs. In the end, you are going to design what you need.

There are benefits to purchasing homes that are pre-built and already thought out. However, the chances of finding the perfect home with everything you want will be slim. You move in, and then you realize, "Well, I would rather the kitchen look like this, or if the bathroom had these accessories, it would be better..." On the other hand, having the option to completely customize and design your home the way you want it may seem like a lot of work, but

> *When it comes to being the best YOU, it begins with knowing your identity.*

in the end, you know you get what you want and need.

Not too long ago, my wife and I faced this struggle. We had all these dreams and expectations, but finding a home that would fill every need seemed impossible. It was the wisdom and guidance of our real estate agent, Robert Paolini, who helped us focus in and figure out the right strategy. I learned that the best plan is to start with the basics, the foundation. That meant we had to identify what was most important in our wants and compare it to what we needed. That became our foundation. We determined what was required, took steps to find those necessities, and only then were we able to add in the other desires.

With the right guidance, you'll learn what you need to survive and what you want to thrive. The process starts with identifying. When it comes to being the best YOU, it begins with knowing your identity.

WHO ARE YOU?

Be who you are and say what you feel
because those who mind don't matter
and those who matter don't mind.

–Dr. Seuss

I always hear people saying that they don't know what they want to do or that they are not happy with their life or career. It's ironic how something that we work so hard to earn can become so dull later on. Is it because we chose wrong? Did we misjudge what would make us happy?

There can be a lot that influences our decisions in day-to-day life. We wonder if our parents would approve of our choices. Would these choices benefit our lives financially, socially, recreationally? Even still, from what are we basing those desires? Did we see someone who was extremely happy while having a lot of money? Maybe we saw someone who seemed very popular, and we seek that same recognition. Perhaps we are so tired of the routine, and we just hope to find peace in a new place. Whatever the case, it comes back to what we want and who we are.

Identity can be very complicated. We spend most of our lives listening to people telling us what to do and who

> *It is easy to let past circumstances hold us back from becoming who we are meant to be.*

to be. It is easy to let past circumstances hold us back from becoming who we are meant to be. Let's start with a question: Who am I? It can be a tough question to answer accurately. Just think, If someone asked, "Who are you?" how would you respond? Go ahead and try, write it down if you need to. Don't stop at just your name; try to dig deep into how you would describe yourself. Now let's take it a step further. If someone asked one of your friends to describe you, would the answer be the same? How about if they asked your parents or a teacher or even a former boss? I think you get the idea. Our identity does not always look the same. The answer may look different based on our circumstances, so how can we know the real answer?

WHO INFLUENCES YOU?

As I mentioned, influences play a significant role in our identity. That means we can't ignore them! Let's start with the question: Who influences you?

Of course, we have obvious influencers like our parents and family. Growing up, they shape our most prominent times of development. You can generally see many of the same characteristics from parent to child. That is why the saying goes, "The apple doesn't fall far from the tree." As we age, our influences broaden to include our friends and peers. We see how someone responds to a friend's jokes or an outfit, and naturally, we want the same attention. We can try to emulate their character, but is that truly you?

These guides are what I would call immediate influences and are directly connected to you. However, those who impact us reach beyond our immediate sphere of friends and family. Now more than ever, we are surrounded by influences through the technology provided to us. Entertainment options, media, and culture are all potential external influences!

The people we watch on TV or through online media are continuously influencing our decisions. We watch videos about what to eat and how to dress. We watch review videos before we make decisions on what games to buy or what products to use. It's terrific that we can now learn so much by typing a few words into a search engine, but it only adds to the point. These external influences have a lot of power in modern-day trends and decisions.

Look at Kanye West when he developed the Yeezy shoes. The shoe concept itself was not a massive new invention, but West's influence caused them to become incredibly popular! For some time, if you had a pair, you were immediately considered cool and wealthy in the eyes of every teenager. The truth is, our identity is often linked to circumstances related to our current look or clothing preference.

> *"A good first impression can work wonders."*
>
> *-J.K. Rowling*

Carol Kinsey Goman, Ph.D., in *Forbes Magazine*, stated that our brains make the most crucial decisions about someone during the first seven seconds we see them. Many people quote Albert Mehrabian's research indicating that 55% of first impressions are made by what we see, 38% is in the tone of voice heard, and 7% coming from the actual verbiage. While some will debate these numbers, it's crucial to keep in mind the power of a first impression.

Think about it: if you show up to an interview at a prestigious multi-million dollar company and you are wearing board shorts and a tank top, do you think that you will be evaluated the same way as someone who shows up in a tailored and pressed business suit? Of course not. Why? Because your identity to the potential employer has been set by your appearance before you speak a word. Does that mean that you are less qualified, talented, or capable than the other candidate? Not necessarily, but it means that your chosen identity may have held you back from that opportunity. Although maybe that wasn't you anyway. If you like to dress that way, perhaps a career based around water is a better fit.

WHAT INFLUENCES YOU?

Let's go beyond who influences your identity. There is a reason you dress the way you do or choose the friends you have. I believe you can find the answer to the question: What influences you?

People can be very influential, but our experiences with those people or even within our circumstances can have even bigger impacts on our identity.

Going into my middle school years was a challenging time. I had just recently moved to a new state. I attended a private school throughout my elementary years, and then suddenly, I was put into public school for my 6th grade year. I was one of the youngest students in the school, and I hadn't made any friends yet. You could say I was starting fresh. This was a clean slate, where no one knew what I was like before my arrival. This allowed vast potential to make a *new* me. I could be whoever I wanted to be if only I knew who that was.

The only person I knew who would be at my new

school was my older brother, who would be an 8th grader that year. He was taller, older, and more experienced with the strange world of middle school. So it made sense to ask my *immediate influence* for advice on how to best survive in this new world.

We went shopping. I was outfitted with fancy tattered jeans that cost way more than they should have and a long sleeve flannel. Then for some reason, I put a t-shirt with a prominent logo repping the name brand of choice on top and rolled up the flannel sleeves to my biceps. Before I knew it, I was the spitting image of a "prep" from an advertisement for an overly priced clothing company. My brother shaped me into the identity of what was currently quite popular.

School started and I did my best to walk the walk that my brother taught me. I looked and acted the part for the first couple of weeks. Very quickly, the "popular" kids invited me to sit with them at lunch and hang out. There was just one problem. I was *nothing* like them on the inside. I grew up at a private school where I was regularly taught to be kind to whoever was around me and to represent myself with moral character. This new group of "friends" seemed to believe the opposite was the best way to live. They would ridicule any students who came by that didn't look like them, and they weren't afraid to insult each other as well! They were not kind to others or themselves.

I won't even get into the moral choices they made. It didn't take long for me to realize this was NOT my identity. If being popular meant being mean to everyone and going against most of what I believed was right, I was happy to be unpopular. And I did just that.

One day I decided to put on my old baggy jeans and a t-shirt from some local store that had a funny picture on it. I noticed a table of students at the opposite end of the lunchroom that seemed different. This group was quite diverse. There were gamers, artists, skaters, kids mixing all their food into one concoction and making bets who would eat it first, and one kid who was rather large and always wore a Scooby-Doo embroidered jean jacket. They seemed like fun, so I walked right over with my lunch and asked to join them. It's probably no surprise, but they immediately welcomed me and introduced themselves. Here, I was able to just be ME.

> *Every time we go through an experience, whether good or bad, part of it sticks with us.*

This personal experience would unquestionably influence my future decisions about who I would hang around, the activities I would choose, and the clothes I would wear. I learned a lot about my identity in those years.

Every time we go through an experience, whether good or bad, part of it sticks with us. An only child might enjoy having more alone time than someone with multiple siblings. Someone who was bitten by a dog may not like being around dogs very much. I watched a young friend who was playing baseball accidentally throw the bat as he swung to hit the ball. He became so embarrassed that he decided that he didn't want to play baseball anymore. These personal experiences can weigh heavily on our desires. On the other hand, we don't always have to experience something to learn from it. When we see or hear stories of different people's experiences, they can equally impact our identity.

I remember several years ago when my brother got a few kittens. His family loved playing with the cats. We were all in his living room when out of nowhere, a kitten decided to turn around and latch onto his wife's face! The claws were implanted just above her eyes and into her cheeks. I remember seeing the blood start to drip from her face as she fought to pull it off. She ended up being okay (and the cat was later declawed). I'm glad that it was not me, but watching it happen still impacted me. Since that day, I have decided that I would try never to hold a cat near my face. I also do not plan on having any cats in my house. My wife is allergic to them, after all.

These types of situations happen all the time: moments

where we see someone go through something traumatizing, then decide we don't want to experience the same thing! I can recall hearing a mother or teacher saying something like, "Don't do *that*, or you might get hurt!" followed by, "I've seen a boy crack his skull by doing just *that*!" It was their own experience that shaped their cautious identity, and they could not help sharing with those around them. It is good to learn from experiences, either our own or someone else's, but we have to decide how those experiences will shape or limit our future identity.

There are a lot of influences that we encounter throughout life. We will discuss some of them in more detail in the coming chapters, but you have to decide: are these influences for better or for worse? Are the influencers that you are letting shape your identity going to help make you the person you want to be, or are you allowing them to bring you into a repetitive trap of following the crowd?

When I decided to stop hanging out with those "popular" kids in middle school, I knew it meant that I would very quickly lose my "good standing" with a majority of the students. As you can imagine, those students were not happy that I left their group. The next two years were pretty rough as they spread rumors and picked on me whenever they could. However, I saw an identity in them that I did not want to see in myself. I chose to get rid of the negative influence and found one that I felt was in line

> *Sometimes you have to let go and get rid of the influences that keep you from being your best.*

with my standards.

It's important to realize that not every influence is there to help move you forward. The more you understand who you are, the more you can separate the good from the bad in terms of influences. I hope to help you see some of the people of influence that are currently surrounding you. Are they improving you and pushing you to be better, or are they dragging you down and holding you back? Sometimes you have to let go and get rid of the influences that keep you from being your best. But the only way you can fully know what's best for yourself is truly understanding who YOU are.

FINDING YOU

Our goal should be to answer this question: What is my true identity? What do I want to do or be? Since our identity just seems to get more and more confusing in the world we live in, let's try to get to the root of who we are.

You have two options:

1. Spiritual route

When asking myself the question "Who am I?" my immediate thought is, "Who am I, but who God made me to be?" I grew up in the church, so for me, I found a lot of my identity in who God said I was. If that is not something you agree with,

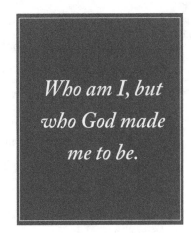

> *Who am I, but who God made me to be.*

you are welcome to skip down to option two. If you are curious, allow me to explain.

Take a look at this painting. If I were to ask you what you thought this was, you would probably have quite a variety of responses. It is not a simple or clear painting, but that is how Picasso painted. How can we know for sure what the art is? How can we have a definite answer? The simple answer is to ask the one who made it. Picasso titled this painting *The Accordionist*, and since he painted it, the identity is only revealed in what he says it is.

Now, let's look back at our own identity. If you want to know your identity, you should ask the One who made you! Now, I am not talking about asking your parents, though I will hit on that in option two. I am talking about God. If you believe that a Creator created you, then that Creator is going to have the best idea about your real identity.

In the Bible, Ephesians 2:10 states, *"For we are His workmanship, created in Christ Jesus for good works, which God prepared beforehand so that we would walk in them."*

So what does this mean? Well, for one, it states that we are not shot out like confetti coming out of a cannon. The word workmanship comes from the Greek word poiēma, meaning: "that which has been made; a work." This word is stating that we are made on purpose. We are something that is worked on over and over again until it meets the intended goal. So if we are God's workmanship, and God is perfect, then we are not random. It means there was specific thought and effort put into making us who we are.

If that is true, no matter what other people say, I can always come back to the foundation of knowing that I am made by God on purpose. But even then, we may still ask why we were made as we are. Why am I short? Why do I look the way I do? But in the end, what matters is knowing that you are who God says you are: His workmanship.

This verse also says that you were made with a purpose to do good things! Not a purpose to fail, but to succeed!

You were made ON purpose WITH purpose. So the next time you feel like you are not good enough, or strong enough, or popular enough, ask yourself this question: Do those things define you? All of those traits are comparative circumstances. They are not limiters to your potential.

> *You were made ON purpose WITH purpose.*

Once again, you are who God says you are! The great thing is, God doesn't imply that you are this completed piece of work once you spend enough time at church, reading, or praying. He said you were created that way, regardless of your background or beliefs! That's pretty encouraging to consider when we live in a world that often tells us that we are not enough.

SIDE NOTE ON BIBLE READING:

It's not always easy to know how to find those answers, so I encourage you to start with the Bible. It's not just some old textbook, but it speaks the truth about who you are. While the Bible can seem huge and intimidating to some, it's worth finding a place to start. No one expects you to simply pick it up and start reading on your own and finish it right away. There are plenty of reading plans out there that help space it out into manageable segments. There are also countless commentaries on the Bible. If I could offer a suggestion, start with finding a translation that you like to read. Since the Bible was not originally written in English, most translations are interpretations from the original Hebrew, Greek, and Aramaic. If you asked me which is the best translation, I would say the one you *like* to read. Then in the future, find yourself a good study Bible that is a close translation to the original languages (like the New American Standard Bible or the English Standard Version). Once you have found the right Bible (or Bible app), then try reading a few verses a day to get started. You can use a "verse of the day" that is pre-chosen for you or pick up a simple devotional book. Once you are comfortable with this habit, then start reading the context of those verses. However you choose to go about it, don't try to do it alone! Remember that there are plenty of people who have studied the Bible for many years. Don't be afraid to ask someone for help understanding what you've read!

FINDING ME

Figuring out my own identity took work. As I mentioned in chapter one, I grew up a pastor's kid, and that meant that people had certain expectations of who I was supposed to be. Some people expected me to know all the right answers and always to do what was right. The other group expected me to fit into the "pastor's kid stereotypes." That meant that I would be expected to misbehave frequently and cause trouble more often than not. Unfortunately, that's just how people view the children of most pastors. I had to decide which of these I would "fit into" if I was to meet the expectation. I'll be honest, when I was in elementary school, I was a bit of both! I remember times I sneaked out of classrooms to go looking for bugs instead of sitting still, but at the same time, I loved to learn about God, so I tried to do what was right.

Being picked on while I was in middle school due to my choice of friends was a challenge. I quickly could have let the name-calling or the way certain people treated me define who I was, but I wasn't convinced they were right. For me, the significant change came when I got to high school. It wasn't the new school that changed me, or even the growth spurt that happened in the ninth grade. The most significant influence on my identity came with choosing to become a part of my youth group at church.

My parents were still pastors and I was still the awkward kid that didn't particularly care about other people's opinions of me, assuming that they would just label me a good or bad pastor's kid again. But there was one opinion that stood out. It was an opinion that I could not ignore. My youth pastor had a phrase he would like to share with the students; "You are a world changer!" He would say this again and again. He didn't only say it from the stage; he would tell it to us one on one. He believed in us. As students, we were young, immature, and unsure of what to do. But he knew one thing for sure: he knew that we had the potential to change the world.

I often thought to myself, "Me? What could I do?" I had not accomplished very much up to that point in my life. I was intrigued. I wanted to see if he was right, so I decided to join the student leadership team. I was given opportunities to use my talents, gifts, and hobbies to make a difference. It started with just helping behind the scenes by setting up for services and events. From there, I began to run the lights and audio. Eventually, I was leading the youth small groups at my public high school. Somewhere between ten and thirty students would gather in classrooms to talk about God and life before school started. Back at the church, I even had opportunities to speak on stage to my peers. I started believing what I had been reading from the Bible throughout my life. I looked at the talents and desires that God gave me and decided to give it back to God. I chose to live by one statement: "If I was going to do anything, it was going to be to give GOD glory."

That changed my perspective of myself. I wasn't living to meet the needs of others, but the more I focused on God, the more God met needs through me. This taught me that *I am a world changer*. Who are you? Who do you want to be? Who does GOD say that you are?

2. Secular route

If you prefer to leave the "supernatural" out of the equation, then let's look at our identity differently.

We mentioned earlier that we have many influences in life. As we grow and mature, our identity and personality become shaped by those influences, whether they are experience or personal interaction with individuals.

As an infant, we are at the mercy of our parents and their choice in parenting style. Our "first impression" of the world is taught to us by our parents. ZerotoThree.org and The Bezos Family Foundation partnered together to survey how soon parents think they are influencing their children compared to the actual age of influence. A majority of the parents thought they had until one to two years of age before their actions significantly impacted their infants. In reality, the study showed that at six months of age and sometimes even sooner, an infant's brain has already begun "building" based on those influences. It's believed that during the first two to three years of a child's life, over 700 neural connections are formed every second. These connections are building and setting the *foundation* of an infant's brain.

That's just the beginning of our lives. We continue to find our identity through elementary school, middle school, high school, and even college. Even after 18 years, our cognitive development is still maturing, and our self-identity is being formed. Many neuroscientists say that we are not actually settled in our development until the age of 25. That just goes to show that we need to put value in what we surround ourselves with.

So think about you for a moment. Your past helped get you to where you are today, but with all that, who have you become? What brings you joy and excitement? What do you find yourself doing with the majority of your time? Is that what you want to spend your time on? If you could plan every day on your own, without any resource limitation, what would you do? Your answer to these questions speaks volumes about your identity. Often, individuals will get caught up in their current workplace, profession, or even their friend group, and that becomes their identity. However, just because someone spends all their time in one place does not mean that place identifies with who they truly are or want to be.

Our identity is truly found in our choices. As adults, we choose what to do, who to be around, and how to live our lives. I accept that there are circumstances that may limit those choices, but in most situations, those

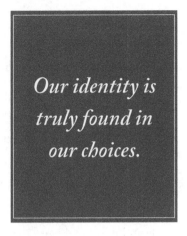

Our identity is truly found in our choices.

circumstances are crafted by our prior life choices. I have been asked, "What if someone was born with a disability or accidentally disabled?" Have you spent time talking with a medalist from the Special Olympics? Do you believe they see their disability as their identity?

Look at the story of Louis Braille. In 1812, at the age of 3, he was blinded in an accident involving an awl (a leather working tool). In that time, the blind were rarely cared for, but Louis and his parents refused to let being blind keep him from learning. He attended a school specifically for the blind. Louis met Charles Barbier, who introduced him to the concept that would later be perfected as the "Braille System" in 1829. Even though the world labeled him as blind and often looked past him, he made a choice to persevere. He invented the method we still use today, for the blind to be able to read and function on their own.

A dear friend, Tom Shill, was born blind. He continues to astound me with his dedication, motivation, and his indomitable spirit. He uses a refreshable braille display to be able to read documents from a screen. This device raises the letters in braille as he scrolls through the text. With this incredible tool, he can lead groups of students through discussion questions sent to his phone in real-time. It is incredible how the students stay focused on him because of his ability to read from the display. He has been serving as a youth leader for over thirty years. He refuses to let being blind get in the way of impacting the lives of students. He sings on stage and has a beautiful voice. He enjoys going on youth trips and camps. He even jumps into rounds of dodgeball and plays Minecraft (a very visual and creative building game) with the students. He knows his identity is not found in his disability, but a willingness to make a difference. He is a leader!

It's time to stop making excuses about our identity and start shaping it ourselves. You can either be best or be like all the rest. You can choose to be great or let others be greater. But it's up to you to define your life.

The more we know about who we are, the more likely we are to succeed at what we want to do. That doesn't mean we will get it right on the first try. We may find ourselves pursuing several paths before we land on the one that truly satisfies our desires.

I know that I want to stay fit and healthy in life, so I have often found various ways to do so. I never liked the mindless repetition many people endure in a gym. For me, I always enjoyed learning while getting a workout. That is what led me down several martial arts paths earlier in life. I recently decided that I was going to pick up the sport of jiujitsu. It seemed exciting to learn how to do grappling and how to handle situations when I could be knocked down to the ground. For seven months, I struggled through a lot of pain and discomfort to learn the foundations of the sport. After that, I realized that my body just did not respond very well to the vigorous nature of the training. But if you asked any person who was in the class, they would tell you that I always gave my best effort. I was exhausted and worn out, but I would give it my all. The important thing to me was not winning every time, but trying my best every time. What I found most challenging was learning how to give my best effort without wasting my energy. My best wasn't in line with being the best competitor, and I had plenty to learn. But even

> *You can either be best or be like all the rest.*

though I knew I was not the best, whenever it was my turn, I would give my best.

Giving your best doesn't guarantee success. You choose what you do and how well you want to do it! Then take the steps described in this book to get there. Your identity is the foundation of being the best you. Yet it's how you chose to build on that foundation that makes progress happen.

Everyone fails at who they're supposed to be...
a measure of a person, of a hero,
is how well they succeed
at being who they are.
–Frigga (Avengers: Endgame)

BEST PRACTICES

1. If you were to give yourself a label, other than your name, what would it be? Try to come up with three answers.
2. Are those answers what you want to be labeled as or something you want to change?
3. Make a list of your daily influences, both good and bad. Which bad ones can be removed first?
4. Does your inner circle of influence help you improve your growth or impede it?
5. Who are the people you can thank for helping get you where you are today?
6. What commonly brings joy into your day? How can you keep those things more present in your daily life?
7. Make a list of qualities you want to be known for. How can you improve those qualities?

USING YOUR BEST MATERIALS

AMBITION, BOLDNESS, AND CONFIDENCE

3

Better ingredients, better pizza.
–Papa John's Pizza

Yes, I just quoted a pizza franchise. And no, this chapter is not sponsored by Papa Johns. What are your thoughts on the quote? Is it true? If I am cooking a pizza and I have "better ingredients," does that mean I will make a better pizza? Well, not exactly. I have to know how to cook a pizza correctly. There is a specific order to the process to make it successful. Having the ingredients available is just part of the process of creating a "better pizza." It is knowing how to use those ingredients that matter. It starts with the basics of making a pizza.

In our journey to build our best potential, the ingredients matter. But so does knowing how to use those ingredients. Wisdom and identity alone won't build you up to be best. It is knowing what to do with your identity and all that wisdom that helps your best take shape. That's not going to happen just sitting down with your eyes closed. It's going to take effort and vision.

I have seen many people try to achieve greatness but fail or give up in the process. Most of them had great ideas (blueprints) but lacked the necessary "ingredients" or materials to succeed. The purpose of this chapter is to explain how to have the best vision. They say "hindsight is 20/20," but foresight can be as well, with the right materials. We will call these materials the vision ABC's: Ambition, Boldness, and Confidence. I want to help you know how to use these materials to make the best results possible. But remember, these ABCs only put the materials in your hands. The following chapters will help you learn how to use them effectively.

Hellen Keller said, "The most pathetic person in the world is someone who has sight but no vision." Helen can seem harsh, but she understood what a blessing it was to have sight. Many have no choice on whether they can have sight. Vision, on the other hand, is a choice. Having the ability to see is good, but it doesn't mean that we always know what to do with it.

My wife enjoys the peacefulness of putting together puzzles. She likes to buy the large Thomas Kincaid Disney puzzles that have vast landscapes and scenes from her favorite movies. When we first start the puzzle, it's a mess. I know that somewhere in the mess there's a beautiful piece of art, but just seeing all of the separate pieces can be overwhelming. My wife, being as detail-oriented as she is, likes to work from the outside edges in. It's a good strategy because there are only so many pieces that have a flat side. Following her vision, we can put together the border of a puzzle in minutes. But once you get to the interior, things get complicated. A new vision is needed. Without that vision, we would just take pieces of the puzzle and try to force them to fit over and over again until it seems like any piece fits. Even though I could force a piece to fit, it wouldn't meet the intended image without a vision of the final product.

Sometimes life can feel like a puzzle. We have work to do, skills to learn, people to talk to, places to go, and somehow we have to find time for ourselves. It's like looking for that one piece of the puzzle that you know is there. You saw it at some point, but you can't find it when you need it. Eventually, you skip it, saying "It will show up later." It's normal to feel this way, and sadly, it's normal to stay that way. Most people tend to think that life must be busy and full, or it's unproductive or unsuccessful. People may say that having a full schedule proves their importance. But that doesn't mean that they are productive with their time. Others may say that it's better than having nothing to do. But we aren't after just "better." To be best, you have to understand the importance of a vision that will produce efficient and effective results.

> *To be best, you have to understand the importance of a vision that will produce efficient and effective results.*

The first material needed to achieve our best final product is ambition.

Ambition:
am·bi·tion
1. a strong desire to do or to achieve something, typically requiring determination and hard work.

I've seen it one too many times. In my career, I get to meet a lot of young teenagers. I believe these teens can accomplish so much at their age, but often they don't feel the same way for varying reasons. What I notice most often, though, is a lack of drive or ambition.

These students usually don't have a lot of responsibility. They are young—why should they? Most adults are hesitant to give young students responsibilities because they believe that the results will be lacking. It's possible, but it is also possible that they could surprise everyone with accomplishing something great! Throughout history, we see many moments where someone young accomplished great things.

• Mark Zuckerberg launched Facebook when he was only nineteen years old, and now is worth billions.

• Fraser Doherty, at the age of fourteen, started making jam. That led to the creation of his "SuperJam," which has sold millions!

• Justin Bieber, at age twelve, started making homemade videos that led to him being picked up by singer Usher. By age fifteen, he was already going on tour with Taylor Swift. Just ten years later, in 2019, his net worth was estimated to be over $285 million!

• Katie Stagliano, at just nine years of age, grew a massive 40-pound cabbage for a school project. What is admirable about it is that she used it to feed 275 homeless individuals. In the next ten years, through "Katie's Krops," she dedicated her time to her dream of helping people. They donated over 38,000 pounds of produce to people and families in need.

What do you think would have happened if the adults and influencers in their lives just said, "No, they don't need the responsibility. They are just kids, let them relax..." Without responsibility, their potential goes to waste.

When someone young accomplishes something, even if it may seem small to us, their minds enjoy the feeling of success! They begin to crave more success. They start to believe in themselves. They take steps to see how they can succeed in other areas. The feeling of success can drive someone to try something new and accomplish something even more significant. In other words, the results of those small responsibilities will develop into an ambition to do more. It's this drive that can help a student become their BEST.

Some of the proudest moments in my career as a pastor have been seeing students realize their potential when they are just coming into their middle school years. I've seen some of these young students take on extraordinary challenges and succeed!

One day we challenged our students to see how they could impact the community for the better. We listed off several ideas and concepts that they could run with and then encouraged them to give it their best, regardless of their age. One would expect the oldest students to do the best, but that wasn't the case. One of our 6th grade students, on his way home from church, noticed a homeless man. After remembering the challenge, he decided on his mission! With the support of his family, he started a campaign to raise money to help the homeless in his community. His first step was to make lemonade. He began to sell lemonade on the side of the street to help raise funds to support the needy. The word started to spread, and soon the local news caught wind of what this young student was accomplishing. In the end, this student raised over $3,000 and donated the funds to an organization that provides transitional housing for homeless families! Here was a young middle school student who was doing his best to make a difference. He believed that he could, and with his ambition, he began the hard work to accomplish his goal.

Ambition requires hard work! Simply put, if you're lazy, those ambitions will fade away, and you'll find yourself just getting by instead of living your best life. This is procrastination. In college, procrastination was a challenge for me. When you are living on campus with friends available at every hour of the day, it is difficult to dedicate the time needed to do the work well. I even had a "motivational" poster above my desk that had a boy sitting on the edge of a beautiful lake, and underneath it read, "Procrastination: Hard work pays off often, but laziness pays off now." Sure, it seemed true, and I had some great times with friends, but halfway through my first semester, my grades were nowhere near what I needed them to be to keep my scholarships. I realized that I had to change some habits and take down the poster that "motivated me" in the wrong direction. I needed to work hard to get my grades up, but more importantly, to learn the necessary skills for the career path I had chosen. Once I learned the value of working hard, I found out that it allowed me more quality time with my friends without the overbearing burden of procrastinated work. Working hard isn't an easy path, but it is the path with the biggest payoff. If you want to achieve the best ambitions, be prepared to work hard, take the right steps, and pursue the best results!

There are two steps to best utilize your ambition. The first is **dream big**.

> *If you can dream it,*
> *then you can achieve it.*
> *-Zig Ziglar*

What is your ambition? What do you want to accomplish? If you want to accomplish something incredible and life-changing, it will require some dreaming. Start thinking about what you want to achieve. Is there something that gets you excited? What are you passionate about?

If you don't know where to run, you may just run the wrong direction, or you may stop running entirely. Having a dream gives you something to chase after. Maybe you have heard someone described as "a Jack of all trades but a master of none." Sure, it's nice to be good at doing a lot of different skills, but there are always people who will be better—people who chase a dream to be best.

If you haven't figured out your dream yet, that doesn't mean you have failed. Don't forget, at some point, your dreams may change! The journey toward your dreams is what will help shape you into your best.

When I was young, I had dreams of being a scientist.

I wanted to study insects, reptiles, and amphibians. My dad taught me how to identify and catch snakes at an early age. I remember catching my first snake on my own at five years old. I knew it was a harmless ringneck that I had found under a rock, but that didn't keep me from getting scolded for picking up a snake so quickly. My parents were cautious because they knew that snakes could be dangerous. But instead of being fearful, I was fascinated and wanted to know more. I asked for books that would help me learn about insects and reptiles. I would catch and raise them, as I learned how to care for them. I was chasing my dream! At least, it was my dream as an elementary and middle school student. Eventually, my desire to see if I could breed a praying mantis and a dragonfly (which I still think could be an interesting experiment) faded to the background of stronger ambitions. In high school, I felt a very clear calling that I was supposed to go into ministry or church work. It was different than before when I just thought that a particular subject was neat or intriguing. This time, I felt like I had a purpose that was bigger than myself. I wanted to pursue this new dream, but it took time. I did not know where to go or what to do with this newfound ambition. That led me to step two.

The second step to best utilizing your ambition is to **make a plan.**

*Every great dream begins with
a dreamer. Always remember, you have
within you the strength, the patience,
and the passion for reaching for
the stars to change the world.*

– attributed to Harriet Tubman

Dreams are great to have, but if you can achieve
your dream without any planning, you probably are not
dreaming big enough. It is possible to get lucky, but luck
should not be relied upon. Big dreams will yield big results,
but those results are typically locked behind a series of
manageable steps and careful planning. If you dream of
flying like the Wright Brothers did, you can't expect to
just jump off a cliff and fly. I hate to break it to you, but
that won't end well. They
took a LOT of time carefully
planning the details of how to
make their dream come true.

First, grab a pen or pencil
and sheet of paper, a napkin, or
even your notes app. Second,
take a moment to visualize
your dream.

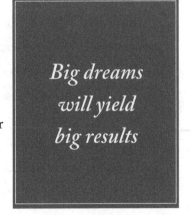

*Big dreams
will yield
big results*

Then write down these three questions:

1. What will it take to get there?
2. What are the small steps you can take now?
3. What are the big steps you want to take later?

It is okay if you don't have every detail planned out. Just jot down the answers to the best of your ability. Consider this a brainstorm.

The first question is just to get thoughts out there. Think of what knowledge and resources you will need. Where will you need to go? What will you need to do? Just empty every idea you can onto this list. Don't worry. You won't get every detail figured out right away. That's what makes it a big dream. Over time you will refine and add to this list.

The second question is more specific to the immediate. You won't be ready to knock out everything on your list right away. Begin by organizing your thoughts into a step-by-step list of what you *can* start on. There are a lot of methods you can use to do this. I have always been fond of the "SMART" process for coming up with goals. I did not come up with this format, and there are many variations you can find online about it. In short, it stands for: Specific, Measurable, Attainable, Relevant, and Time-bound. Are the steps you are planning simple enough to accomplish without overwhelming you? Are you able to measure your progress? Are the steps something that you can achieve from where you are? Are they important to you, and do they push you forward? Are you able to set a time limit to keep you from laziness or procrastination? Keeping these simple questions in mind should allow you to make realistic steps that you can accomplish in a reasonable timeframe.

When I was trying to figure out what direction to go in my own life, I knew I needed help. As a high school student, I had no idea what steps to take, but I was fortunate enough to have good mentors in my life that helped me shape the process. One significant influence was my web design teacher in high school, Mr. McCauley. At the time, I enjoyed making graphics and web sites, so I put a lot of effort into that class. What I didn't expect was that the teacher was more than a web design teacher. Over time I found out that while he taught web design in school, he was also a graphic designer. He also told me that while he enjoyed his work, he was most passionate about youth ministry. He was doing exactly what I wanted to do! I started planning how I could both fulfill my calling and enjoy my hobby. Since it was my senior year of high school, I knew an important part of that plan would be to figure out where I would go to college.

It was not an easy decision to make. I knew that if I

wanted to make good money, then going to a prestigious graphic university would set me up for that. But at the same time, I knew I was being called into ministry. As the time approached, I had to make a decision, and I decided to make a bold one.

The second material needed to achieve our best final product is boldness.

Boldness:
bold·ness, /bōldnes/
1. willingness to take risks and act innovatively

There are risks and costs to action. But they are far less than the long-range risk of comfortable inaction.
-John F. Kennedy

Risk can be scary. It is easy to want to stay within comfort zones and safety, but are we really chasing our dreams if we are not willing to take bold steps to get there? We currently live in a day and age where we are encouraged to think outside of the box and live differently. I will admit this has had some positive and negative results.

We have seen inventions and accomplishments that only seemed to be true in movies and fairy tales. We have also seen people completely go against common sense in the name of "uniqueness." Maybe it can seem like too much for you to imagine changing the world with your dream (or perhaps you're ready to dive in and take on the world), but we also tend to fear being ridiculed for the risks we take. So, how do we find the balance? How do we take bold risks that make a difference without crossing over the lines of foolishness?

> *Are we really chasing our dreams if we are not willing to take bold steps to get there?*

A good starting point is to look at what everyone else is already doing. Just because everyone is doing something one way does not mean it is the right way or the best way. Look at how people normally open bananas. Who would have thought that we have been opening them upside-down most of our lives!? (If you are not sure what I'm talking about, search the "right" way to open a banana.) In life, we are constantly riddled with the "right" way to do things. But maybe "normal" shouldn't be the standard we stop at. Normal is very likely not the best way, but instead the accepted way.

> *Just because someone says "no way" doesn't mean there is NO way. It merely means that those people cannot see a way.*

One of my favorite quotes is from Dave Ramsey about money and how to save in an age that pushes you to spend. He states, "If you live like no one else, later you can live like no one else." It means that sometimes we must think differently, act differently, or dream differently so that we can see the best that may be hiding behind the normal. Thinking outside the box is a crucial trait of bold thinking. Just because someone says "no way" doesn't mean there is NO way. It merely means that those people cannot see a way.

When the Wright brothers started pursuing their dream of flying, people couldn't see what they saw...a way. They didn't know what that way was just yet, but they believed it was there. Flying was not a new idea during the era of the Wright brothers. In other countries, there had been reports of aviators flying via self-propelled balloons. But to fly in a machine that was heavier than air—that was an idea that the general public had a hard time swallowing. After all, several scientists had already published articles explaining how it was impossible and extremely dangerous!

But instead of getting discouraged at the opinion of the majority, the Wright brothers poured into their life's work—to make a flying machine. They were not aeronautical engineers, but that did not stop them from following their passion. They did not let their setbacks and glider crashes discourage them. They took them as learning opportunities to make their machine better. Eventually, their efforts paid off when in front of a small crowd at Kitty Hawk, Orville Wright flew in a plane for 12 seconds over 120 feet. And then, just to show that it was not a fluke, they flew three more times that day, each trip longer than the one before.

Everyone loves a story where one person takes a risk and accomplishes the unthinkable or makes the impossible, possible. You have to decide if you have the boldness to let your dream be one of those stories. Will you settle for normal, or will you pursue the best? We can't let ourselves be trapped, thinking that the "best" has already come; we can always improve.

Music is an excellent example of thinking outside the box. Not just the type of music we listen to, but how we listen to it. From Gregorian chants to devices that send the musical vibrations through your mouth, the act of listening to music has come a LONG way! I remember the days of having a walkman on my side and trying to go for a run or skate with it playing. It would skip every time I hit a bump or crack in the sidewalk (and that was with the "anti-skip" technology).

Enter the iPod. Steve Jobs had the vision to try something new, something bold. He was willing to take the risk to make it happen. Music wasn't new, but he believed that it should be more available. Sure, he could have just picked up cassettes or CDs, but that wouldn't cut it. The iPod was not the first portable music player, but it became the new standard. It is believed that without the innovation of the iPod, we wouldn't have the all-too-popular iPhone today. As an innovator, Steve Jobs was a huge proponent in making the accessibility shift we have with music.

Steve didn't settle for what people had in the box already. He believed there could be better, and he strived for the best! It did not matter if people thought he was crazy. He knew that the results would speak for themselves. His boldness changed the way the world listens to music!

When I was deciding on a college, I had one goal in mind: I wanted to do whatever God wanted me to do. I believe that He had the best in mind for me, so if I could figure out what He wanted me to do, I knew I would be at my best. I weighed the options. I considered which job I would be able to get with which degree. Graphic work tends to pay well, but ministry work, not so much. It was a tough decision to make.

In the end, I looked at my goal and said to myself,

"If I want to know what God wants me to do, I need a university that would teach me more about Him and His will for my life." So I decided to go to a Christian university and get a degree to do the ministry that I knew God had called me to. After that, I planned to go to a graphics university so I could get a degree that would support me financially. It was a bold step of faith. I knew that it was not the easiest option, but I trusted that God would provide. In the meantime, it was my duty to do my best, no matter where I was at or what I was doing. I had to be confident in my decision.

All our dreams can come true if we have the courage to pursue them.
-Walt Disney

The third material needed to achieve our best final product is confidence.

Confidence:
con·fi·dence
1. a feeling of self-assurance arising from one's appreciation of one's own abilities or qualities

Therefore, do not cast away your confidence,
which has great reward.
Hebrews 10:35

Confidence is not something that comes easily to everyone. The "foundation" we built in chapter two can significantly affect our confidence, but to truly have this type of confidence, we need to believe in our identity. If there is anything that can sap away confidence, it is self-doubt and negative influences.

One thing I love about being in my position as a pastor of middle school students is watching the incoming 5th graders get ready for middle school. Most elementary schools stop at 5th grade, meaning at around ten years old, they get to be at the top of the class! Just imagine the feeling. Your age just hit double digits! You are most likely taller than every other student in the lower grades. You have completed all the "elementary training" needed to take on the world. You've got this!

This excitement and confidence are astounding! It can help a child overcome incredible obstacles. During the summer before they "officially" start middle school, they are faced with two choices. Either embrace the confidence and get excited about what's to come or switch into worrying about going back to the "bottom of the pack." What I have noticed most often is, unless these young students are told they do not have to start over from the bottom, they will naturally choose to worry. Society does not speak well of the "middle school years," and that can be intimidating. Suddenly, the "I've got this" mentality turns into "I can't do this." But what happens when you encourage these young students to believe in themselves? What if they held onto that incredible strength found in confidence? The results, from what I have experienced through my profession, are remarkable. These students become capable of incredibly more than expected or anticipated. They don't treat these "middle years" as the worst, but instead, they become their best!

Most likely, you are already past middle school, and maybe you did not have someone to encourage you to do more and stay confident. That does not mean that you cannot start today. I want to tell you straight up, "You've got this!" The fact that you are reading this book is proof enough that on the inside, you have the potential to be best!

A key strategy for high confidence is remembering your identity. That's why it's our best foundation. Believing in yourself will jumpstart your potential to succeed. If you hold onto the truth of who you are, not just what the world says or wants you to think, you are going to find the strength to do your best in the midst of the worst!

There are three obstacles to be wary of so that you

don't lose your strong momentum and deplete your confidence. The first is letting others influence your attitude negatively.

Have you ever walked into a room, and everyone was in a joyful mood? If you have, you know it is hard not to start to feel the same way. At the same time, have you ever watched a movie where the actor or actress begins to cry due to a sad situation? Internally, even though the situation does not affect us in real life, we start to feel the same emotions. Tears begin to well up, and next thing you know, you're reaching for tissues. This reaction is called emotional contagion. If emotional contagion affects our laughter and sadness, you know it will affect our aggression, doubt, stress, fatigue, and fear. It has been tested again and again by various universities. When you walk into an argument, and everyone is yelling and hurling insults, it is difficult to stay in a positive mood. If you are about to try new food and everyone else already exuding adverse reactions, it is more likely that you will subconsciously dislike the food. It's precisely why when feeding vegetables to a child for the first time, we say things like, "Mmmm, it's good, see!" as

> *Seek the encouragement, embrace the critic, but always remember your potential.*

we gulp down disgusting split pea soup. Our emotions are contagious, so we need to use caution about what emotions we surround ourselves with!

Your potential success is not stifled by your past, but rather, it's held in the grasp of your present willingness.

When you are surrounded by people, even just one or two, who discourage you, then you are just wasting potential energy. When you have someone telling you that you are going to fail, you start to believe that. Instead, surround yourself with people who are like-minded and who will encourage you to push past your limits!

This does not mean to ignore constructive criticism. We need people who are honest with us about how we can improve. If you ignore that criticism, you are ignoring wisdom that may guide you to the best ways to improve. Seek the encouragement, embrace the critic, but always remember your potential.

The second obstacle is your past. Just like with identity, our past can weigh significantly on our confidence. If you grew up in an environment that always brought you down, then you might still believe those words. Words can have incredible lasting effects on our mind's efficacy. While your past is an excellent teaching tool, it is essential not to let it hold us back from our future. Times are constantly changing, meaning what may have been true in your past may not be true now. Your potential success is not stifled by your past, but rather, it's held in the grasp of your present willingness. Don't let your past hold you back. Instead, pursue your future ambitions!

The third obstacle that often saps our potential confidence is failure. I am not talking about your past failures, but the failures of others. More than likely, someone else has tried to achieve what you are aiming for. Some may have succeeded, but many failed. Those failures can be like taking a drowsy pill before participating in a sporting event. It's just going to bring you down.

In my hobby of parkour, there are a plethora of "fail videos." It is a sport that takes a significant risk and has a lot of room for potential error or extraordinary feats. Because of this, people are continually recording these "watch this!" moments. If you go online and search "fail" or "bail," you will find an excess of videos that could potentially leave you laughing or wincing in sympathy pain. You might even find footage of my friends and me from our early days. These videos are what feed phenomenon shows like *Americas Funniest Videos*, but what does watching all those videos do to your mind?

When you see someone fail you either laugh it off,

or you put yourself in their shoes. It is the emotion that causes us to cringe and say, "Ooh, that had to hurt." That moment plants a seed in your mind, that grows into a tree and blocks your way. I have seen this happen to myself, and many friends and trainees in parkour. Right before they get into a position to attempt a move, they suddenly stop and say, "I don't know." At

> *Learn from mistakes, be confident in your potential, and then take your best leap forward. You've got this!*

that moment, I turn to them and say four simple Spanish words: "Tu cabeza esta mal," which means, "Your head is wrong." I say this to remind them that the hindrance is not in their physical potential, but instead is a mental obstacle. Sometimes we can't help but have these little doubts, but we do have control over how many seeds we plant in our minds. There is nothing wrong with a bit of laughter and entertainment, but if we dwell on failures, we are only adding to the list of obstacles in our minds. Learn from mistakes, be confident in your potential, and then take your best leap forward. You've got this!

The vision ABC's are each important on their own, but it is the union of all three that can take someone from good to great, from better to best! How far will your ambitions go without boldness or confidence? If you have boldness but lack confidence and ambition, where will you go? If you have all the confidence, but no ambition to pursue with boldness, will you be productive? Having the best vision requires all three. George Washington Carver said, "Where there is no vision, there is no hope." I believe that there is a specific reason that you are aiming to become the best that you can be. I don't know your story, but I do know that hope will play an essential role in your journey. Let your vision lead you to that hope, and then make it a reality!

BEST PRACTICES

1. If you could make one wish to make the world better, what would it be?
2. What is one thing that you've always wanted to accomplish in your life?
3. What are the obstacles keeping you from fulfilling that dream?
4. What small steps can you take to start working towards your dream?
5. What negativity needs to be transformed into a positive perspective?
6. How can you keep your future goal more prevalent than past failures, whether yours or someone else's?
7. Set some reminders to help keep your eyes on your goal. These can be physical or digital reminders.

GAINING YOUR BEST
MOTIVATION

PURPOSE

4

Leadership requires two things:
a vision of the world that does not
yet exist and the ability
to communicate it.
–Simon Sinek

About four years ago, I had the vision to start writing my very own book. It was right before my wife and I planned to go on a cruise. I thought this would be the perfect opportunity to "get away" and write. On the first afternoon, I went to the top deck, sat out in the sun, and started writing. It was a thrilling moment; I was finally beginning to write my book! I wrote down a ton of ideas and thoughts on how I felt the book should go. I believed I was making great progress, and then my wife came over and asked if I wanted to go swimming. The weather was perfect; how could I refuse? Then we decided to get food. After all, why else do you go on a cruise other than to eat unlimited amounts of delicious food? Before I knew it, my "thrilling excitement" got lost in the pleasures of a cruise vacation. The problem was, I lacked a key ingredient to success—motivation!

I just wanted to write because I had some useful concepts that I wanted to share, and I thought it would be a fun project. There is nothing inherently wrong with that, but it wasn't strong enough to win over the continual barrage of distractions and side interests. Because of my lack of motivation, I spent the next two years sporadically feeling motivated enough to write a few sentences, paragraphs, or maybe an occasional brainstorm. My great intentions and ambitions were going to waste because of a lack of motivation. My day job as a pastor over students kept me very busy and worn out. I didn't have enough energy to pursue any form of intellectual self-dialogue that would lead to good writing. After a while, I thought of a new way to get the motivation going. I started taking steps forward. I bought the domain names and email addresses that would eventually be the landing page for the book. If I were going to spend money on these little things, then maybe I would feel the pressure to get it written. Unfortunately, that wasn't the case. I needed the best motivation, but I was adding some leaves to the fire instead of adding actual firewood that would last and endure beyond the distractions and excuses. I did not have enough weight in my motivation.

If you want to succeed at achieving your dreams and ambitions, you're going to need the right motivation. I want to use this chapter to clarify the motivations you need to have the best results and keep that fire going. First, let's look at some inadequate examples of motivation.

MONEY

It never fails that I see someone start some new endeavor with hopes and dreams of becoming rich. There is nothing wrong with wanting to have money. Money can play a significant role in seeing some ambitions through to completion. But the problem with money as a motivator is that it's never enough. It comes and goes. Once you feel like you have what you need, you see someone else with something bigger and better, and you think to yourself, "If I had more money, I'd have *that* too." In reality, money is hardly ever the actual motivator for our work. Typically our desire for money comes from a false appetite for other lacking motivators. People often seek money to gain status, to find pleasure, or even in pursuit of affirmation. Don't let money be the only force driving you forward.

POPULARITY AND STATUS

This one took some self-reflection to figure out. One of the original reasons I wanted to write this book was to help show that I have what it takes to be a communicator. After many years of being in the same profession, I wanted to show that my position was not the only thing that defined me. This desire was a good motivator, but in the end, it was still too shallow to fully keep me going.

We all want to be known for something great. No one goes to school with the hopes of being entirely unpopular. Naturally, we want people to like us! A desire for popularity drives people to be seen and approved of on social media. But are those truly the results we want? Are they going to satisfy the internal desires we have? Like with money, what is the real reason for wanting to be popular or gain status? This desire may have something to do with our foundational identity, but by itself, it is not likely to carry us across the finish line.

SELF-GAIN AND SELFISH AMBITION

Behind money and popularity, you often find selfish ambition. Instinctively, we have a desire to take care of #1. When we focus on our personal needs or desires, we can easily forget that we are not the only ones with needs and desires. Telling yourself that your dream will make your life better can be exciting, but there are many ways to make your life better. How might your ambitions make your life better? Will they be worth the personal effort if someone else can just do it for you? There is a common phrase often said to procrastinators: "If you don't do it, someone else will." This usually proves true! When self-gain is our motivator, procrastination could set in until, eventually, it's too late. Your dream has already become someone else's reality. Rather than becoming a driving force, these moments can become quite demotivating.

Having hints of these possible motivators will not leave you in the wrong. Some of them might even be good at times. Although I don't think your goal is to settle for just good. Hopefully, by now, you have a desire to go beyond good and reach for best! So what motivations can lead us down the best path and pursuit?

SELFLESS NATURE

Have you ever had one of those moments when your adrenaline jumps into overdrive? It seems like everything in the world slows down. As our body's nervous system kicks into gear, our adrenal gland delivers cortisol and adrenaline into our bloodstream. Suddenly, strength limitations seem to fade away as our muscles prepare for action. Nothing stops you from accomplishing what's in front of you, no matter how impossible it seems. It is in these moments where normal humans become like superheroes. Throughout history, people have sought to take full advantage of this phenomenon. It's why so many people pursue dangerous adventures and daring acts. But, what if I told you there is a more accessible way to achieve these unbelievable feats than standing on the edge of a skyscraper or mountain cliff?

Some of my favorite stories to hear about are moments when you see people do superhuman feats for others' sake. One excellent recent example was the feat of Zac Clark, a 16-year-old boy from Butler, Ohio. CNN and Fox both report that Zac was doing yard work with his mother when they heard a yell for help. Rushing over, they found a 39-year-old father trapped underneath a 3,000-pound car that had fallen while he was working on it. By human standards, this 16-year-old boy should not have been able to lift the vehicle. But something welled up inside of him. Zac had lost his father the previous summer, and he wasn't willing to stand by and watch someone else lose theirs. Miraculously, Zac lifted the car enough for the man to escape, whether by adrenalin or sheer motivation. In one article, they reported Zac saying, "He had a couple of cracked ribs, and his face was messed up pretty bad, but the doctors told him if I wasn't there, then he'd be dead. I just thank God for putting me in the position and giving me the strength to do that."

These "superhuman" stories are not bound to comics, fairy tales, and superhero movies. They happen more than many people realize. The common thread is almost always an act of selfless nature and someone willing to go beyond the limitations of reality because of the motivation to help someone else. While researchers are still unable to explain

> *One of the biggest keys to unlocking the best strength is learning to think and act outside of personal gain.*

these situations with 100% confidence, we know that throughout history, people have been able to accomplish much more than initially believed to be possible when properly motivated.

One of the biggest keys to unlocking the best strength is learning to think and act outside of personal gain. Often I hear the argument that this strength will only work for "loved ones," but if that were true, how could someone pick up a car to save the life of a stranger? The simple answer is to learn to have a love for life and those in it! If you have an appreciation for life and the people that are in it, you will find working for those people much more desirable, and in return, you will tap into a new strength. Most people would agree that love is a powerful force. That is why most stories and fairytales revolve around it. So what will it take to tap into that powerful force? How can we use it to motivate us to work beyond ourselves for the betterment of other people?

In the church, we call this servant leadership. It is a concept modeled after how Jesus served the disciples who were following Him. The symbol was during the last supper when He got down and washed the disciple's feet, even the one who He knew would betray Him later that night. I could go into detail about how their feet were dirty and the importance of feet washing, but what's important is that this leader got down and did what the servant would usually do. Selfless love showed those disciples, and us, that status should not limit anyone from caring for other people, whether friend or foe.

If you want to push beyond your limits, work longer than you think you can, and achieve the best outcome, then seek motivation beyond yourself. Start thinking about the people who can benefit from your work. Will your dreams and ambitions improve the state of your family? How can your ideas change the world? This type of selfless thinking is precisely the type of motivation that can push you through the challenging moments. No one likes letting people down. As we mentioned earlier, we all seek the approval of others. Yet,

> *If you want to push beyond your limits, work longer than you think you can, and achieve the best outcome, then seek motivation beyond yourself.*

instead of allowing our desire for that approval drive us, let's strive to live a life that automatically provides that.

For this to succeed, we have to learn to love. I have given my students a key verse to live by. This verse, written by the apostle Paul to the Roman church, explains how love should motivate us to serve others and live in a way that improves the people around us.

Don't just pretend to love others. Really love them.
Hate what is wrong. Hold tightly to what is good.
Love each other with genuine affection, and take delight
in honoring each other. Never be lazy, but work hard and
serve the Lord enthusiastically.
Rejoice in our confident hope.
Be patient in trouble, and keep on praying.
When God's people are in need, be ready to help them.
Always be eager to practice hospitality.
Romans 12:9–13

Approach your dream with a perspective of love.

Whatever your dream is, learn how to approach it with a perspective of love. If your ambitions only benefit you, you are less likely to follow through. This perspective will drive you to do more than you thought possible, pulling out the best in you!

ATTITUDE

While learning to serve others can be a powerful driving force in your efforts to do best, attitude is a critical factor in being able to serve consistently.

In 2 Corinthians chapter 9, Paul writes to the people of Corinth the importance of giving with the right attitude. He states, *"Remember this: Whoever sows sparingly will also reap sparingly, and whoever sows generously will also reap generously. Each of you should give what you have decided in your heart to give, not reluctantly or under compulsion, for God loves a cheerful giver."* He continues to explain how this attitude makes a lasting impact on the world we live in. When we handle our motivation and drive with the right attitude, the labor necessary becomes an exciting process as opposed to a resentful drag.

POSITIVITY

I know that sometimes, positive thinking has a "negative" connotation. As I mentioned before, I'm not trying to sell you on the idea that you can physically fly into the sky using will-power alone. However, with the

> *Positivity is about more than just achieving a singular dream. It is about a lifestyle that says "I'm not giving up."*

right attitude, you can adapt to your surroundings and learn to fly in a new way. Positivity keeps you from giving up, even when things aren't going your way. It also allows you to push forward after moments of negativity and failure.

This mindset is about more than just achieving a singular dream. It is about a lifestyle that says "I'm not giving up." Science and history have proven time and time again that there is power in positivity. When we think positive thoughts, our minds naturally release the chemical serotonin. This chemical causes us to feel better, calmer, less worried, and capable of focusing more. It's hard to do our best if we feel bad, anxious, or stressed. All these feelings drag down our productivity. So if positive thinking can eliminate these emotions bringing us down, why wouldn't we aim to be more positive? It is good to be realistic; however, it is best to look at what's realistic from a positive perspective.

I love this quote from Zig Ziglar: "Your attitude, not your aptitude, determines your altitude." We often want to "climb the ladder of success," but people tend to assume that skill is required to get there. Let's say you were about to hire a new employee, and you had two candidates. One has a lot of schooling and an impressive resume, yet in the interview, he was rude, arrogant, and seemingly unhappy. On the other hand, the next candidate did not have an incredible resume, but you could tell he was willing to learn and take on whatever challenges were ahead of him. Which person would you rather have for the job? Someone who has a positive attitude will often learn from mistakes and breed more positivity in the workplace. He may not know every skill up front, but he is willing to take the time and effort necessary to learn. This type of attitude is more likely to deliver success. It is not always easy to see it, but keeping calm and positive is more likely to drive someone to improve. Thinking positive does not mean you won't have failures, simply that you will handle failures better. You may actually grow from them.

So how can we maintain this positive attitude that drives us to the best results? There are countless books, classes, and videos that claim to have all the secrets to happiness. I have nothing against them, and I think many of the methods they suggest can bring positive results. I believe that the root underneath these methodologies derives from a couple of simple virtues.

FAITH

Faith is often attached to a religious meaning or purpose. While faith is essential to most religions, the essence of faith is the foundation of a positive lifestyle, regardless of religion. If you looked up the definition of faith, Merriam-Webster defines it as "something that is believed especially with strong conviction." While I like that definition, my favorite description of faith comes from a letter written to the Hebrews dating back to the first century.

> *Now, faith is the assurance of things hoped for,*
> *the conviction of things not seen.*
> *Hebrews 11:1*

How often do we look at a situation and wonder how it will resolve? Will the results be beneficial, or will it become a detriment? This unknown is the moment when we have to decide what we believe. We may not see the outcome in certainty, but we have hope for a particular result. That's faith believing in one outcome to happen.

To have a positive outlook, it takes faith to believe that positive results will ensue regardless of what we can currently see. It means, even though things seem to be going downhill, you look past that and aim for potential growth. Once you take that aim, you push forward with a strength that comes from believing that the effort is worth it! The question is, are you willing to chase after what you don't see yet? If the answer is no, then you are slipping towards the opposite of faith—doubt.

DOUBT

Doubt

/dout/

1. A feeling of uncertainty or lack of conviction: uncertainty of belief or opinion that often interferes with decision-making

Did you notice that the definition states that doubt "interferes with decision-making"? Often people have doubts, and then they stop moving forward. They let doubt interfere with potential success. The problem is not having moments of doubt, but instead, allowing doubt to halt your progress. Doubts are just moments where you must decide what you believe. Do you believe in what you are working towards? Do you believe that it is worth the effort? If so, when you face those doubts, let them remind you of the faith you hold in your motivation. Let them drive you forward instead of hold you back. The best results derive from having positive faith in those doubtful moments.

The problem is not
having moments of doubt,
but instead,
allowing doubt to halt your progress.

HOPE

For faith to be effective, hope is required. Hope is built on faith. Faith is the belief in a particular result. Hope is the excitement coming from that positive belief, which drives us forward. It is the moment when you realize the outcome is worth the effort. Having hope changes the way we see life. Hope absolves worry and allows us to overcome adversity.

> *Hakuna Matata.*
> *It means no worries.*
> *–The Lion King*

We can all hear Timon, Pumba, and Simba singing "Hakuna Matata" from *The Lion King*. It's an iconic moment where Simba learns to be less focused on his unfavorable past and finds hope in a brighter day. In the movie, it's an interesting point in Simba's life where he must decide what to have faith in. The presence of faith creates an absence of worry, thus "hakuna matata."

Worry is something that seems to plague so many individuals. It is often defended under the guise of safety or caution. People make excuses to avoid action because it seems like more than they can handle, but is it too much? It's wise to be safe, but if you put that in front of your ambitions, you'll find yourself missing out on the best results. I am not saying you can't have fear, but what's important is knowing how to face it. We'll discuss this in more detail in chapter six.

The question is, how does worry help? Growing up in church, I spent a lot of time reading the Bible. I've noticed that the Bible says quite a bit about worry. A few of my favorite verses were:

Worry weighs a person down;
an encouraging word cheers a person up.
Proverbs 12:25

So do not worry about tomorrow; for tomorrow
will care for itself.
Each day has enough trouble of its own.
Matthew 6:34

Don't worry about anything;
instead, pray about everything.
Tell God what you need,
and thank him for all he has done.
Philippians 4:6

These verses represent that worrying is not worth it. All it will do is slow you down. Instead of worry, overcome your concerns with hope in the results! Being positive and encouraging will give you the strength to overcome those worries. Having faith and hope in each moment will help you surpass your fears to arrive in the next moment. Some of these moments will be scary; some will be challenging; some may be downright overwhelming. Yet, in those moments, "hakuna matata": hold onto your hope in your future!

What is your motivation? What are you so passionate about that it will drive you to do your best? Yo-Yo Ma said, "Passion is one great force that unleashes creativity, because if you're passionate about something, then you're more willing to take risks." Life without risk is not truly living.

Nearly every action we take has a level of risk involved, whether it is stepping out the door, getting in our car, or having conversations with people. In chapter one, we learned about the wisdom we gain from experience and guidance. With that wisdom, we can confidently take on the risk because we have learned our identity and what we are capable of. Now, even when we feel tired or discouraged, we can

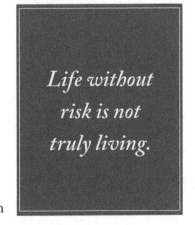

Life without risk is not truly living.

confidently chase our dreams and overcome any fears or worries by having faith and hope. It's time to push forward and achieve what's best!

BEST PRACTICES

1. Have you ever started a project but ended up walking away from it or forgetting it? What happened?
2. What are your biggest motivators? Write them down and keep them visible as a reminder.
3. Who is someone you hope to help?
4. Who are the most positive people you know? How does their positivity affect their success?
5. What do you need to put more faith in to keep you from doubting?
6. Write a list of what worries you. How many of these can be overcome by what you've learned in this chapter?
7. What success stories can you find to remind you of how capable humans can be? Make an "inspiration" folder!

BUILDING YOUR BEST TEAM

UNITY OVERCOMES LONELINESS

5

*The challenge of leadership is to be
strong, but not rude; be kind, but
not weak; be bold, but not a bully; be
thoughtful, but not lazy; be humble, but
not timid; be proud, but not arrogant;
have humor but without folly.*

–Jim Rohn

As an ordained pastor, I have the honor of officiating weddings for couples ready to take on the incredible adventure of marriage. In almost every wedding ceremony I mention the verse from the Bible, Genesis 2:18, where God said, *"It is not good for the man to be alone."* At the beginning of the creation, God says that everything He created was good, except one thing. God noticed a vital detail: we were not designed to be alone. We see in the scripture that God created Eve to be with Adam, to be a partner beside him.

Another verse that is used often in wedding ceremonies is Ecclesiastes 4:9-12. Whether you believe in the Bible or not, it's hard to argue with the truth in this verse. *"Two are better than one because they have a good return for their work: If one falls down, his friend can help him up. But pity the man who falls and has no one to help him up! Also,* if two lie down together, they will keep warm. But how can one keep warm alone? Though one may be overpowered, two can defend themselves. A cord of three strands is not easily broken." Often, we are forced to be on our own, but those are moments of potential growth by bringing to light the value of a team.

Maybe you think you are alone, or you don't need help. Perhaps you've tried to form a team, and it didn't work out well. This chapter will help you bust through the myths of the lone wolf and see the value in team unity. It will also help you gain an understanding of how to grow your team. Being best doesn't mean being lonely.

> *Often, we are forced to be on our own, but those are moments of potential growth by bringing to light the value of a team.*

YOU'RE NOT ALONE

MYTH #1: Do it yourself!

You have probably heard the saying "If you want something done right, then do it yourself!" This is usually said after a delegated task fails. The prevailing thought is that individuals are better off doing something on their own than getting help, because other people may not do an adequate job. While parts of that may be genuine to an extent, it is a shallow view of productivity and far from the best approach. How many tasks can you give all of your time to before you get worn out? What happens when you approach an obstacle in an area where you do not have the necessary knowledge? Will you take the time to learn a new skill for that task while still completing everything else that is necessary?

These are questions I had to ask myself as I got more involved in my path of ministry work, specifically when I started in youth ministry. I essentially had to learn the "ins and outs" of an entire company. I had to plan intriguing events and craft inspiring programming that kept the attention of middle school students each week. I had to design current and trending advertising and graphics. I became the lead recruiter seeking out leaders and volunteers. I would deal with external family conflicts and handle administrative tasks while trying to write theologically sound messages that could keep my audience's attention. Youth ministry taught me to be good at a lot of diverse tasks, but I could only go for so long before my performance began to decline.

I remember reading the story of Moses and the Exodus of the Israelites. Moses was brought up in a household that taught him many essential skills for leadership (see Acts 7:22); however, handling the entire civilization was a daunting task. In Exodus 18, we see the wisdom from his father-in-law, Jethro. Take a look at verses 13-23:

"Moses took his seat to serve as a judge for the people, and they stood around him from morning till evening. When his father-in-law saw all that Moses was doing for the people, he said, "What is this you are doing for the people? Why do you alone sit as judge, while all these people stand around you from morning till evening?"

Moses answered him, "Because the people come to me to seek God's will. Whenever they have a dispute, it is brought to me, and I decide between the parties and inform them of God's decrees and instructions."

Moses' father-in-law replied, "What you are doing is not good. You and these people who come to you will only wear yourselves out. The work is too heavy for you; you cannot handle it alone. Listen now to me, and I will give you some advice, and may God be with you. You must be the people's representative before God and bring their disputes to him. Teach them his decrees and instructions, and show them how they are to live and how they are to behave. But select capable men from all the people—men who fear God, trustworthy men who hate dishonest gain—and appoint them as officials over thousands, hundreds, fifties and tens. Have them serve as judges for the people at all times, but have them bring every difficult case to you; the simple cases they can decide themselves. That will make your load lighter because they will share it with you. If you do this and God so commands, you will be able to stand the strain, and all these people will go home satisfied.

When I read this, it was like a light suddenly turned on. I realized I was just wearing myself out in my job. I was forcing myself to get everything done on my own, no matter how much time it took or how much work was needed. It was the "best" I could do... at least that's what I thought until I read this scripture and realized there had to be a better way. I started recruiting talented volunteers and delegating specific tasks. At first, I had a tough time letting go of tasks that I knew I could do very well, but I had to tell myself that I didn't need to be the one to do them. I would delegate a task then see results that didn't seem as adequate as what I would have done, and it would upset me. If the results were not the *best*, then I wasn't pleased. These moments led to making a few mistakes when communicating with volunteers, and I found myself returning to re-do those tasks.

It was in these moments that I learned that I was not alone. While it wasn't my father-in-law who showed up, my wife noticed the strain on my work and shared her insight with me. It was a learning process of letting go of tasks and being okay with the time it took to build up others in the skills that I once mantled alone. Now, as I fast-forward nine years, I can see the results, and they indeed are much better than what I could have accomplished on my own. Not only is the ministry thriving, but my emotional

> *If you want something done best, don't do it alone—build up a team that can support you and takes you further!*

and physical state is also improving. This book wouldn't have been possible if I was still trying to do everything on my own.

The truth is, we are NOT better off alone. We were designed for community: not just for moments of delegation, but moments of laughter and sharing, hardship and grief. Our mental state is better off with other people involved. Yes, there is risk involved with allowing others in, but we already discussed the necessity of boldness if we want to achieve our best. If you want something done best, don't do it alone—build up a team that can support you and takes you further!

Myth #2: It's lonely at the top.

In many businesses and careers, people believe the more successful you are the more lonely you become, in part because those people think that others can't keep up or will slow them down. Another thought is that other people feel inadequate or unqualified, so they distance themselves out of fear. Sometimes it's because people who work their way to the top may become so filled with pride that they push other people away. Regardless of the reason, one might believe "being lonely at the top" is a definitive statement. However, each of these viewpoints can be overcome.

Inevitably, bringing in someone new will slow progress; but with proper discernment and leadership, it will eventually allow for increased speed and development. For that to work, though, the leader has to be willing to lead with the individual. At first, that individual may feel intimidated, maybe even afraid of making a wrong move. A good leader does not invoke fear, but leads with love and encouragement. That doesn't mean letting people usurp authority. Maintaining the balance of firm leadership while encouraging growth

> *A good leader does not invoke fear, but leads with love and encouragement.*

and improvement is key to developing new leaders. It allows individuals to learn from mistakes and grow to more exceptional potential under said leadership.

CareerBliss CEO Heidi Golledge mentions, "Happiness can impact productivity, employee loyalty, and overall employee success." So why would we not want our employees to be happy? Many highly successful companies commonly place a high value on happiness in the workplace. Companies like Nike, Chevron, Google, Adobe Systems, Starbucks, and Apple all have high regard for their employees' approval ratings. Why? Because the best leaders care about other people and their happiness.

The other day I was in an Apple store when suddenly I heard an eruption of clapping and cheering in the already bustling store. I quickly asked what was going on and found out that one of their employees was leaving. The employee that I was talking to noticed the look of confusion on my face. He explained to me that they believe the same level of excitement and celebration showed when making a new hire should also be given when some leave to a new workplace. They believe the employee will be moving on to continue to grow and make the world better. As the employee made it through the 30-person cheering line, she had joyful tears in her eyes while walking out the store waving. Everyone present could feel the positivity and felt lighter due to the caring nature of her co-workers.

It was evident that every employee there mattered and that they were not alone in their work, but supported by everyone on the team.

The most significant cause of feeling lonely at the top is a leader's attitude. It's the attitude they have toward others, toward themselves, and their work. If a leader treats others with contempt, then the workers won't feel valued, resulting in them not valuing their work. If a leader swells with pride and arrogance, others will come to dislike him and eventually work against him. If a leader sees their work as a burden that no one else can help carry, they will distance themselves from those who are capable of offering the most support. When the *Washington Post* asked the CEO of Apple, Tim Cook, about the difficulties of being CEO, he mentioned, "The real problem facing CEOs and top leaders is not loneliness but rather isolation." Many leaders claim to be lonely, but it's often because their decisions lead to isolation. In reality, it's only lonely at the top if we choose to go alone.

> *It's only lonely at the top if we choose to go alone.*

The best leaders realize that being best doesn't mean being alone and isolated. There are times when it is appropriate to find a quiet place and get away for some solitary space. However, that's balanced with finding times to be with people who drive you further and encourage growth. Even Jesus, who is recognized as the most influential leader in history, found it necessary to have moments of solitude. He was often seen going into the wilderness, or mountainside gardens to pray and be alone. You can find a few examples in Mark 6:30-32, Matthew 14:1-13, Luke 6:12-13, Luke 22:39-44, and Luke 5:16. But outside of those moments, we see Him continually leading leaders. Not everyone agreed with Him but His potential to influence, even to this day, is undeniable. If you think about how many songs, paintings, books, articles, and conversations are based on Jesus, His leadership is clear to see. Being best is not a solo gig.

A leader should aim to build a life based on service, not a career based on advancing up the series of positions.
–James M. Strock

THE VALUE OF TEAMS

Once someone accepts that being alone is not best, it's essential to make sure they put the best people around them. In Chapter 1, I quoted "show me your friends, and I'll show you your future" which is a familiar quote that I have heard repeated by numerous pastors and leaders. I believe there is a lot of truth in this statement. If you look at the people you allow around you and, therefore, the ones influencing you, you will have insight into what your future may look like.

What that means in the pursuit of the best life is that we need to surround ourselves with the best people. The higher the quality of the people around you, the more likely those people will improve your quality. That doesn't mean that you can only surround yourself with people with fancy degrees and qualifications. Quality is about more than qualification. Many people are more than qualified but lack actual quality.

On the other hand, some people may seem completely unqualified, but they possess the dreams, drive, and foundation necessary to surpass limitations. Often, this second group of people just needs a leader who can discern their quality and lead them forward. When you build up your team, look for people who have the qualities that you know will propel you forward, encourage your dreams, and challenge you towards growth. Not everyone has to be exactly like you. A diverse team can most often help you see things from various perspectives and facilitate new growth, but having a team that can unite in vision is crucial.

We are more capable when we are with others. We see this often throughout history. Many of the most influential people in history chose to surround themselves with positive influences and critics who brought out the best in them. One flaw that I see often is watching a leader make enemies out of competitors or people with different perspectives. Those leaders choose opposition over cooperation. Making enemies will only lead to isolation while learning to have healthy rivals can drive you further. Instead of pushing away people who think differently, we can learn to utilize those viewpoints to find the best potential path.

As we look for the best people to help drive us to the best life, we have to ask ourselves who pushes us forward. It's essential to lead people to their potential, and it's also vital to have rivals who motivate us to try harder. A critical role to fill is the one who is pushing you to be more than you thought you could be. This individual could be a mentor, a coach, a boss, or even a good friend. But whoever it is, they need to be honest with you and help maintain accountability. I am referring to the person who knows where you want to go and is ready to be straight with you about your focus or progress. They may keep you from falling behind or push you to aim for the next level. They will help prevent you from making mistakes that could impede your progress or even talk you through errors that can become learning moments. No one is too good or too qualified to ignore this part of their team. You may have to be bold in asking someone to take on this role. Some may even pay for it to ensure it's the quality they are seeking.

> *When it comes to our time and attention, some of those people deserve it, some take it, and others need it.*

However you find this person, make sure you rely on them and trust them to be honest with you. Be open with them about your doubts, worries, fears, and goals. Don't be angry when they are hard on you. And most importantly, be sure to thank them for helping you in your journey to being best!

After you find the right people to put on your team, the next step is to continue to grow your team.

We encounter a countless number of people every day. When it comes to our time and attention, some of those people deserve it, some take it, and others need it. As you learn who falls into which category, you can start to recognize the people who can help grow your team. We want to have the best team, so we have to learn to find the best people. It is important to surround yourself with people who complement your skill set, and not with people who only tell you what you want to hear. Similarly, if the people around you are tearing down your dreams and crushing your hopes, they are not the best people to be around.

Keep in mind, you don't want to give up on people who are different or lack the right skill set. Those people need direction and guidance as well, even if they don't realize it. One example of surrounding yourself with these types of people looks like the standard 360-degree leadership model: one person above you (the mentor), one beside you (the rival), and one below you (the apprentice). Over time, as your circle grows and the quality of those around you improves, your "apprentice" may become a leader too. The best leaders equip other leaders to be best, which means you have to be willing to help make others better than you!

I said earlier that a leader is only lonely at the top if he or she chooses to go alone, but what happens when we decide to bring others to the top with us? As more people reach the top with us, there are now more top-performers, leaders, and best-givers. A big part of why I wrote this book is to help make that happen. I strive to see a movement where, more often than not, people give their best in every situation! I can only imagine what our world would look like if more people gave their best effort in everyday life. I believe there would be a rise in innovative inventions, incredible achievements, and other life improvements through this positive change. I believe that YOU are a part of that movement.

*The best leaders
equip other leaders
to be best,
which means
you have to be willing to
help make others
better than you!*

BEST PRACTICES

1. Do you consider yourself a leader or a follower? Who are you leading, and who are you following?

2. List out the qualities that you believe make a great leader. How does your list compare with what culture shows?

3. Who are some of the most successful leaders you know? What makes them successful?

4. Who in your life could benefit from your leadership? What can you teach them?

5. Who is draining your time and restraining your growth?

6. Identify a "rival" who could push you to become a better leader.

7. Think about the people you interact with the most. Are you raising new leaders?

ENSURING YOUR BEST REINFORCEMENT

STRENGTH IN STORMS

6

*The closer you get to the mountain top,
the harder the wind blows.*

–Daredevil (TV Series)

I've lived in Florida for the majority of my life. While we don't have many "mountain tops" we have plenty of strong winds, specifically of the hurricane and tornado variety. Multiple times, my family's home withstood the eye of a hurricane, and we even had a tornado sweep through our property. Storms are real and they can be scary to face, especially if you're not used to them.

I remember a time as a child when we were coming home from church on a rainy, windy day. As we approached our street, we noticed what looked like a shed in the middle of the field adjacent to our property. Then we saw our neighbor in the street, under a bright umbrella, waving and pointing at the field. We noticed that the fence to our back yard was flat on the ground, and something was missing from our yard: the shed. It was our shed that was hurled across the street and into the field about 100 yards away. It turns out that a tornado went right through our yard, but only knocked down our fence and took our shed. The rest of our home and belongings were just fine. We thanked God that our family and home were both okay. We fixed the fence and recovered what was in the shed. The situation could have been so much worse.

That was my first memory of dealing with the intense Florida weather. It taught me a valuable lesson: reinforcements matter! If you don't want your stuff to blow away, you must reinforce it to handle the storms. Now, as an adult owning my own home in the stormy, I mean the Sunshine State of Florida, I have to be prepared to deal with the storms on my own. When we heard that a hurricane was on the way and was heading straight for our home, my first thought was, "I need to secure and reinforce the shed!" I had just built the shed that year, and I was not going to have it blow away like the one in my childhood memory! I added stakes, tie-downs, chains, and several bottles of "Great Stuff" to make sure that the shed would stay standing and in place. I probably overdid it, but I wanted to be sure my work would not blow away in the storm. Thankfully, it worked! After returning from evacuation, everything was where it was supposed to be, with only a fence knocked over and a downed tree.

In Chapter 1, I mentioned the story of a house built on sand to demonstrate the importance of our foundation. As important as a foundation is, there is equal importance to being connected to that foundation. In Florida, there are specific building codes and requirements that must be met before any construction of homes or buildings. While most days there is a gentle breeze over the oceans and the sun is shining, we also have a pretty consistent hurricane season. It makes sense that these regulations are in place to prepare structures for the storms that may come. Before the storm ever arrives, precautions and reinforcements are put in place to ensure the stability and safety of the structure.

When I was in college, I had another learning experience about reinforcements before a storm is even a thought. I earned a Chrysler Sebring convertible from my parents when I was a senior year in high school. It wasn't a fancy car, but in Florida, it was nice to take down the top and enjoy the weather. I had the top down almost every time I was in the car, no matter the forecast. I kept hats and blankets in the car to keep my passengers happy. Due to how often I put the top down, it began to wear out. Occasionally, when it rained, water would leak in at certain spots. As a college student, I did the wise thing: I put a towel under that spot and thought nothing of it. It seemed fine at first. However, one day while driving with friends, it began raining so hard that the leak became a downpour that needed to be taken care of immediately! The problem was, it was the middle of the storm. I had towels and blankets, and as every man should, a roll of duct tape in the trunk. I pulled underneath a large tree and attempted to tape over the gaps. Unfortunately, the top seemed to be getting worse by the second. The problem was, everything was wet! The tape wouldn't stick to the damp surface, so my efforts were going nowhere. In the end, my passengers and I were soaked, my car was soaked, and all we did was add a lot of tape residue and mess to the car. Needless to say, after the storm passed, I had a LOT of cleaning and apologizing to do. I could have avoided the situation if I took the precautions to reinforce, repair, and secure the top before the storm.

In this chapter, the focus will be on how to reinforce the structures of your life. This practice will help prepare you to be ready for the inevitable storms of life. Don't wait until the storm is already overhead to protect what is important to you. If you have read this far, I believe that your future, purpose, and ambitions are meaningful. So protect them from the storms. Learn to grow stronger to overcome the worst and achieve the best!

REINFORCE YOUR LIFE

At this point, you have already started figuring out what is important to you. With an understanding of what holds value in your life, you can begin learning how to reinforce those valuables to ensure no storm will take them away. At some point, there will be a storm in your life, whether it is related to your dreams and passions, your loved ones, your personal belongings, or even your self-esteem. The question is, how do you respond to those moments? Do you look at these storms and give up? Do you let them overwhelm you and eventually overtake you? Do you face them on your own or with help? Do you run from them or toward them? You may not know the answer to some of these questions if you have not been through many storms. However, understanding how to respond in a challenging moment is often the key to overcoming it.

Recently I acquired my scuba diving certification. I have always loved exploring. The idea of being able to explore and see what no one else has seen has always been a dream. Amazingly enough, there are still vast amounts to be discovered underwater. The process of getting certified was pretty lengthy, and I quickly learned there was a lot more to diving than just holding my breath and swimming. I had to learn the science behind breathing air while underwater, and how to properly manage that air so that I would not injure or even kill myself in the process.

An important part was learning to breathe continuously and consistently. Now that may seem simple, but when you are underwater and suddenly see your first shark swim by, it's not so simple to be "consistent" in breathing. Of course, the natural response is fear and shock. Your breath becomes quick and heavy, and you wonder if you are going to die. This all happens, of course, before you find out it's just a nurse shark that would probably never harm a human. Understanding is essential, and knowing what to do in those moments can save your life. We are instructed in moments of panic or worry to follow these crucial steps:

1. Breathe   2. Think   3. Act

It's vital to continue to breathe to avoid damaging your lungs underwater. In the training session, they teach you precisely what to do in many emergencies, so it's important to think back to what you learned. Once you have the right solution in mind, it's time to put the plan into action. These simple steps have saved thousands of troubled divers from various problems, life-threatening and not.

The certification process helped teach me the importance of understanding how to react during challenging storms in and out of the water. There are plenty of moments where life throws a sudden curveball, and no one wants to fail in those moments. Unfortunately, all too often, we let those storms keep us from fulfilling our ambitions. So how do we adequately prepare ourselves for the coming storms of life?

WHICH IS GREATER?

A pretty common story that we hear in church is about how the Israelites escaped from Egypt to get to their promised land. In this story, we can see some valuable life lessons on how to overcome storms. The book of Numbers, specifically Numbers chapter 13, recounts a portion of the Israelites' journey, where we find them at the edge of their promised land. It's called the "promised land" because, for many generations, the land was promised to the Israelites. You can imagine the excitement to be right at the door of something you've heard about your entire life. As they get ready to enter the area, Moses is directed to send spies into the land to prepare the way. Moses chooses spies, one from each tribe of Israel, and sends them ahead as instructed. These spies enter and explore the land. Upon their return, they give this report: *"We went into the land to which you sent us, and it does flow with milk and honey! Here is its fruit."* In other words, this land was rich and plentiful. It was ripe for harvest, precisely what they needed! This land was a promise from God, and they saw that the promise was real! Unfortunately, that's not all that they saw. The next verse says, *"But the people who live there are powerful, and the cities are fortified and very large."* They saw promise and noticed that there would be some problems along the way.

> *Which of these would be more significant, the problems or the promise?*

At this point, the traveling nation of Israel had a choice. Which of these would be more significant, the problems or the promise? Two of the twelve spies immediately spoke up and said that they should go seize the land. These two believed the promise from God was the greater option. Unfortunately, the rest of the people were terrified and chose to make the problem a greater choice. Both groups saw the same thing: a beautiful land full of promise and problems that would not be easy to overcome. So how come the two spies were able to see the current situation so differently? Most likely, it was because of what they knew and experienced in the past.

The nation of Israel encountered quite a few problematic moments leading up to this point in time. They had just escaped from 400 years of affliction and slavery in Egypt. They witnessed and endured ten plagues until the current Pharaoh let them go, only to change his mind and chase after them. As their back was up against the Red Sea, they had to rely on God to help them escape. At this point, God worked through Moses to part the Red Sea and they crossed, escaping the Egyptians. Once on the other side, this entire nation of people had to pass through the desert. Most scholars believe that there were 4-6 million Israelites on this journey. How do you find enough food and water for that many people in the desert? Once again, they had to trust and rely on God to get them through. We read that God provided manna, bread, and quail for them to eat as well as water. What we see is that this was not the first problem Israel had to face. These two spies believed that if God was able to take care of them before, he would take care of their future problems too. They believed that the promise was the best choice to hold on to.

In this story, we find out that the rest of the Israelites gave in to the problem. They were ready to run back to Egypt instead of taking a chance in the promised land that they had been waiting for. They had all the reinforcements they needed, but they never attached them to the foundation that was in the promise. The entire generation missed out on entering the promised land, except for the two spies who believed. Those two spies led the next generation into the land with an understanding that you don't overcome your battles. Instead, struggles can be overcome with reinforcement. For them, the reinforcement was their belief and trust in God.

In our daily lives, we have the same choice to make. What's going to be greater: our problems and storms, or the promise? That promise may be a personal commitment to living the best life. It may look like pursuing your dreams and ambitions. In the end, you can choose how to respond to each moment. You can choose to utilize your team. You can choose to overcome and succeed. That doesn't mean the choice will be problem-free and comfortable, but sometimes we have to get out of our comfort zone to grow.

GET IN THE RIGHT ZONE

When it comes to problems in life, often the goal is to avoid them entirely. Of course, life feels better without problems, but our goal should not just be to feel better. We are aiming for the best. Is living in our "comfort zone" really best?

There is no way to guarantee a genuinely problem-free life. Sometimes, the pursuit of such a life will drive us to live safely in our comfort zone. In the comfort zone, we often feel like we don't need reinforcements. We are comfortable believing that we are safe and that no storm is going to disrupt that safety.

There is a common misconception that being safer is always better. While there are plenty of benefits to taking the safe route, that choice also limits opportunities for growth.

> *While there are plenty of benefits to taking the safe route, that choice also limits opportunities for growth.*

We will often have to learn from a distance if we are continually making a safe and comfortable choice. We are not learning from our own experiences but through the stories of other people. Learning is still happening, but most would agree that the fastest way to learn is from experience.

Imagine watching someone who has grown up reading books about flying airplanes and watching movies about being a pilot getting into the pilot seat of a commercial passenger airplane for their first flight in the air. No one would allow that! Why? Because before someone would be trusted with the lives of others, they have to learn firsthand how flying works in a smaller capacity.

It might be more comfortable to just watch the videos and read the books, but unless we get out of the comfort zone, we will be limited in our potential. Going through hurricanes and storms was not my goal growing up, but after learning first hand what it was like to be in a storm, I was prepared to reinforce my future. To be clear, I'm not saying that everyone should take on the career of a daredevil that chases life or death situations, but we should not just choose to live in a padded room for the rest of life. To find the best reinforcement, we should learn to find a balance of comfort and risk.

> *To find the best reinforcement, we should learn to find a balance of comfort and risk.*

Risk can be scary and cause a quick transition into the fear zone. In Chapter 3, I explained that our doubts and worries could sap away our confidence. It's easy to let that fear of failure or danger keep us from learning. Fear in itself is not entirely negative. So often, people are looked down upon for having fear when, in reality, a healthy dose of fear based in wisdom, can do wonders for our success. That fear might just be the driving force that jump-starts adrenaline and launches us into new territories of knowledge and experience.

In the face of fear, we have to decide what to do next. Do we run back into our comfort zone, or jump into an opportunity to learn something new? To choose the best path in the face of fear, we need to keep those fears in perspective. What do we know about the situation? What have we learned about our potential? Is this an obstacle that requires a detour, or an opportunity to overcome and reach new heights? Celia Luce said, "A small trouble is like a pebble. Hold it too close to your eye, and it fills the whole world and puts everything out of focus. Hold it at the proper viewing distance, and it can be examined and properly classified. Throw it at your feet, and it can be seen in its true setting, just one more tiny bump on the pathway to eternity."

When you find yourself in the fear zone, remember to have confidence in your identity, lean on wisdom, and get rid of excuses. Every moment is a prime opportunity to learn. It is often said that knowledge is power. When it comes to your life, you want powerful reinforcements that

> *When you find yourself in the fear zone, remember to have confidence in your identity, lean on wisdom, and get rid of excuses.*

can handle the storms.

Your goal should always be to **live in the learning zone.** It's never too late to learn. Before a challenge, learn the surrounding circumstances. In the middle of a challenge, read the situation, and decide the best course of action. If you fail, learn why. Ask yourself, "What went wrong, what could I have done better, and what was outside of my control?" If I succeed, learn why! Ask yourself, "What did I do right, what should I remember for next time, and how can I repeat the success?"

In life, we will face storms. Problems will come, but knowledge is our best reinforcement. The more we live in the learning zone, the more we are capable of overcoming our storms. When we learn to overcome, we expand our comfort zone. It's a never-ending cycle where we push ourselves to go beyond our past limits to find our best potential.

Dear brothers and sisters,
when troubles of any kind
come your way, consider it an
opportunity for great joy.
For you know that when your faith
is tested, your endurance has a
chance to grow.
So let it grow, for when your
endurance is fully developed,
you will be perfect and complete,
needing nothing.
James 1:2–4

BEST PRACTICES

1. What are you afraid of and why?
2. Where might you be so comfortable that you are limiting your growth potential?
3. What excuses have you made in the face of an obstacle or storm? How will you overcome those?
4. What negative experiences have you been able to turn into learning moments?
5. Which zone do you find yourself residing in the most: the comfort zone, the fear zone, or the learning zone?
6. Make a list of your biggest failures and successes. Write out what you did right and what you did wrong during these moments.
7. What are some "reinforcements" you can put in place to be prepared for future obstacles, specific to your goals?

LEAVING YOUR BEST LEGACY

DESIGNED FOR GROWTH

7

> *Whenever you do a thing,*
> *act as if all the world were watching.*
> *–Thomas Jefferson*

You've reached the final essential! Hopefully by now, you have a good idea about where to find wisdom. You have a grasp on who you are and what you are capable of. You have decided on a solid concept for where you want to go and how. You know how to build a team to help get you there: a team that will encourage you to push beyond what stands in your way. So now that you feel like you are reaching your best, what happens next?

As Thomas Jefferson said, "Act as if the whole world is watching." If you knew that everyone was watching your life and accomplishments, would that change your choices? The truth is, people are watching. No matter who you are, there are always people who are impacted by your actions. Are those impacts positive or negative? The real question is, what type of *legacy* are you leaving?

Earlier I mentioned that, as an ordained pastor, I am blessed with the opportunity to officiate weddings. Sometimes, I also hold the responsibility of conducting funerals. Typically, funerals are either considered a celebration of life or memorial service, depending on the choices that were made during that person's life. I explain the importance of choices through reading a poem written by Linda Ellis, "The Dash."

I read of a man who stood to speak at the funeral of a friend.
He referred to the dates on the tombstone from the beginning to the end.
He noted that first came the date of birth and spoke of the following date with tears, but he said what mattered most of all was the dash between those years.
For that dash represents all the time they spent alive on Earth, and now only those who loved them know what that little line is worth.
For it matters not, how much we own, the cars, the house, the cash.
What matters is how we live and love and how we spend our dash.
So think about this long and hard; are there things you'd like to change?
For you never know how much time is left that still can be rearranged.
To be less quick to anger and show appreciation more and love the people in our lives as we've never loved before.

*If we treat each other with respect and more
often wear a smile-
remembering that this special dash might
only last a little while.
So when your eulogy is being read, with your
life's actions to rehash,
would you be proud of the things they say about
how you lived your dash?*

I find this poem to be an eye-opening truth. What legacy do you want to leave? How do you want to be remembered? What type of impact on the world will you leave behind?

When I think about these questions, it drives me to refuse mediocrity. I want to be known for doing my best in every endeavor. Not remembered for the wrong choices, but honored for the positive impact I've made. I want my "dash" to be celebrated when the day comes to leave this life behind.

So what can I do to leave that sort of legacy? How can I leave a positive impact on this world in my lifetime and beyond? I try my best to look back at other leaders who have done just that. The most significant example I know of is the life of Jesus Christ. Whether you believe in Him as the Son of God or just a man in history, His legacy is irrefutable! In only 33 years, he left a legacy that is known by most people in the world today, 2000 years later. His teaching helps people to follow two essential values: love God and love people (Matthew 22:37-39).

It may not feel comfortable to love people all the time, and maybe you don't have a desire to love God, but the pursuit of being best means taking on some challenges that may be tough and accepting things we don't fully understand. Jesus' life had such an impact because of his ability to love people. It didn't matter if the individual was rich or poor, disabled or healthy, famous, infamous, or unheard of. Jesus loved them all the same.

He is best described as a servant leader. His goal and purpose in life were to serve others, and He led multitudes! There is a myth that says, "serving others means letting others walk all over you." From the outside perspective, it may appear that way, but the impact servant leadership has on the people you serve is irreplaceable. Showing others that you care about them can quickly change one's attitude toward you. Showing respect will, over time, garner respect.

Jesus understood this and showed it frequently. The most memorable example was when He chose to wash the feet of His twelve disciples. It was a dirty job generally given to someone in a very low position, but Jesus, the leader of the group, chose to do this Himself before having His final supper with them. Why? Because He wanted to leave a legacy that showed the value of loving people.

With a life so filled with love, it's no wonder why He is celebrated every year by people around the world on Christmas and Easter.

Being a servant leader does not mean saying yes to everything, always rushing to help every person you see, and never putting value in your time. When you say yes, say it with a purpose. How can you help them long term? If you answer yes to every little thing, you end up disabling others from their growth potential. There is a time to serve, a time to teach, and a time to lead. You have to find the balance to figure out which one is right for the moment you are in.

A prime example of this is often seen on mission trips. People often go out of their way, spending money and resources to help others in need. This can happen locally or around the world. The goal is to leave a positive impact wherever they go.

I've seen these trips take all sorts of forms. Some groups go out and feed the hungry, some clean messes (natural or not), and do construction projects like building, painting, etc. There are many variations based on the need, and each can have a different impact, some lasting longer than others. It begs the question, are we helping in the best way when we go on these trips?

The most effective mission trips I have seen all involve teaching. If a community requires food, people can quickly deliver food to them. However, how much more helpful would it be to teach them how to grow or acquire food on their own, even after the help leaves? Of course, the individuals being supported have to be willing to put in the effort, but that's on them. In the end, teaching will always outlast simple giving.

Recently, my wife and I went on an overseas mission trip that utilized this concept. The location (not listed to protect their safety) was in an area of the world where religion is heavily discriminated against. As much as we wanted to share with the people our relationship with Jesus, we were legally unable to. So we took a different approach to help this community. We partnered with the local church and worked on meeting their needs. We were told they needed musical training to improve their worship music environments. We planned to arrive with instruments and teachers to show how we lead worship at our church. We all know that music is powerful. It can change one's attitude, set the mood, build energy, or calm the soul. In an area that was so burdened with negativity and discrimination, we believed that music would be a powerful tool to have!

As soon as we met the local group, we realized this trip was not going to be a one-way teaching experience. The congregation and its leaders were so excited about making a difference in their community. They were also already incredibly talented with music and production. It was evident that we would be learning a lot too, and that our teaching plan would need to be adjusted. The good thing is that we were all prepared to be flexible and open to any shifts in the program to help meet the need in the area.

We were able to get to know the worship leaders there. We excitedly shared our songs, and we learned songs in their language as well. As we spent time with them, we learned that music was only part of what they needed. They longed to build relationships and learn how to have conversations that could lead to real change in their lives. It was such a fantastic experience to share their burden with them. We may not live there, but as we built relationships and shared experiences, we began to understand that this trip would amount to more than just a couple weeks overseas.

To this day, we continue to keep those relationships and make ourselves available to partner together to bring hope to their community. What happened was more than just dumping of resources and information, but a legacy that went so much further than the small group that went to help. The leaders, volunteers, and families that we met were ready to continue bringing hope, not just to their community, but wherever God led them. Our legacy had nothing to do with our capability, but our availability. I don't personally believe that I was "qualified" to lead a music seminar, but I did believe that God would put together the right people (not just on our end, but also in their community) to help in the best way. That is what happened. The legacy was not only our own but a shared vision with a community wanting to make a difference in the world.

> *Are you trying to be "better" than everyone else or just trying to be the BEST you? Remember, the best you will make others better.*

Leaving a powerful and lasting legacy is more than just merely helping others. A legacy is also about how we carry ourselves. We can help people but be jerks about it. While the help will be appreciated, that legacy will not bring about positive emotions. It is in those moments that an internal self-check should be made. Ask yourself why you want to help others. What do you hope to accomplish? If you are only helping others to further your "status," then it is not out of love. Are you trying to be "better" than everyone else or just trying to be the BEST you? Remember, the best you will make others better.

People will inevitably look up to someone who helps other people. They become role models for future generations. The best friendships are generally made through caring relationships, not bought by power. When you serve others, it shows that you care about their future, and in return, you will be remembered for it.

People want to know that someone cares. If you think about it, everyone is looking for love. It is no wonder there are millions of songs about love, relationships, or the pleasures associated with feeling loved. Although, this seemingly endless search for love just shows how difficult it is to understand the complex nature of love. One of my favorite resources to comprehend how love works is the *Five Love Languages* series by Gary Chapman. He describes how love is received differently based on an individual's "love language." People attribute the feeling of being loved to one or more of the following categories: quality time, words of affirmation, gifts, acts of service, and physical touch. If you want to help people feel cared for, then understand what is important to them. You can speak compliments all you want to a friend, but if their "love language" is not words of affirmation, you may just be wasting your breath. Find out what action is more valuable to your friend. Do this by testing each option out over time, or just be

> *If you want to leave your best legacy, showing that you care is essential.*

straightforward and ask. Asking how you can best love and care for someone reinforces their appreciation of you. You are humbling yourself to find out how to help them improve.

As a leader, if you want to leave your best legacy, it is vital to show you are not just in it for yourself. If you have individuals under your leadership who do not feel supported and cared for, eventually, they will seek new leadership. There is a delicate balance between showing love and showing strength that leads people to grow under your leadership. Whether you are leading a group of friends, a younger sibling, a spouse, a team, or even an entire organization—if you want to leave your best legacy, showing that you care is essential.

Your legacy will become an example for the people in your area of influence. Do you want them to follow your example? Will it make you proud if they lead as you lead? Because one day, they might!

Being best is not just about accomplishing our own goals, but it means leaving a legacy that encourages others to reach theirs! As we go through the journey and learn how to be our best, we influence others to be their

> *Don't just be the "hero" but be the next guide! Be the BEST guide.*

best. Lead by example. Don't just be the "hero" but be the next guide! Be the BEST guide.

Being best is a choice to live a life that exceeds expectations, overcomes obstacles, and leaves a lasting legacy that makes the world a better place. The journey may be rough, but we grow through the trials and learn to be at our best in the good and the bad. I know for sure that you are capable of doing just that, although it's your choice to take on the journey. If you do, it won't only lead to a better life. It will lead you to the best life. Be best!

BEST PRACTICES

1. What do you hope to be remembered for most?
2. Write down a list of ways that you have been able to help others and how it has impacted your relationships with those people.
3. Do you think people respond positively to servant leadership? Why or why not?
4. Who are the people you will allow to keep you accountable regarding your leadership style?
5. Think of the people you want to lead most. How can you demonstrate that you care about them?
6. Are you happy with the legacy you are leaving, or do you want to improve it?
7. Write down the steps that you are going to start taking to lead to your best life and get started.

FINAL WORDS

NOW, BE BEST

8

As selfishness and complaint pervert the mind, so love with its joy clears and sharpens the vision.

–Helen Keller

BEING BEST IN WHAT SEEMS THE WORST

The year this book was published, critical issues have popped up every month: COVID-19, quarantine, economic decline, murder hornets, humane injustice, riots across the United States, and potential for even more issues before the year is over. However, you can still work towards your best when circumstances seem like they are the worst. Being best means holding on to virtues, dreams, and commitments, no matter how difficult it seems.

Remembering to stay focused on what YOU can do makes all the difference. In reading this book, you have hopefully discovered that you can do so much more when you put your best forward. It requires the decision to make the best out of every situation. I am not saying that everything is always positive and happy. Instead, it takes understanding that when moments are negative and discouraging, finding the best is still possible, although it may require more effort.

Personally, the year 2020 will be one I will always remember. It is the year that my first book was published. It is the year that marks ten years of working at the same church and ten years of being married to my incredible wife. Most importantly, it marks the year that I will experience the love and joy of becoming a father.

My wife and I wanted children for many years. We prayed together, we researched, we saw doctors, and took all the necessary steps, but there was no progress and no reason why. In these hard moments, my wife and I trusted God. We believed that if we were doing our best, we had no reason to be discouraged, and we knew that when the time was right, God would provide. In the middle of one of the most challenging years our country has ever faced, God did just that! He has blessed us with a son of our own. With overflowing hearts, we have decided that nothing can bring us down, as we are choosing to make 2020 one of our best years.

I have always told myself, "If my best is not enough, then whatever it is, it must not be for me." That applied to any job, any project, anything that held value in my life. I can only do my best in any situation. If putting my best effort forward would not suffice, why should I beat myself up for it? Of course, doing my best means I need to follow each chapter of this book. I have to be willing to learn and understand what I am capable of. It would require me to focus my ambitions while being bold and confident to do what is necessary. I would need to stay motivated the entire time. I may have to humble myself enough to seek assistance and get help when I am struggling. And, even when it seems complicated, I would need to persevere, learn from mistakes, and strive for the goal. It is only then I can say that I put my best effort forward, hopefully leading to success. However, if it did not lead to success, why would I be disappointed in myself? I can choose to keep trying or decide when to be satisfied with my efforts and realize that this is just not what I was designed to do.

If you have something on your heart to accomplish, put your best efforts forward. If you fail and it is still on your heart, then don't give up! Keep going through the best steps until you find the success that you are looking for. Don't let failures disappoint you. Learn from them and push forward with hope. If you have learned to trust in who you are, then you can believe that you will find a way!

Choosing the best life means living life differently. I hope that you, and many others, will succeed in finding the best life.

YOUR BEST LIFE

The concept of "being best" is not new, but it can be easy to get overwhelmed. In my journey, I have read and listened to so many books on how to improve my life experience. I make these books a part of my routine because I do not want to miss out on the opportunities that I have in my short time here on this Earth.

I see many individuals say they want to do better in life, but I watch them quit or make decisions that roadblock their progress. I witness countless people make choices that lead to hurt and pain, whether inflicted on themselves or others. This world is full of answers on how to make life better, but those answers must be sought out and pursued. It is not enough to simply state you want your life to be better. You must take the proper steps to get there.

When I see the troubles going on around the world, I have to choose how to respond. I can ignore the problems and isolate myself from them in an endless pursuit of peace, or I can decide to do something about it. I know that I am not capable of fixing all the problems in the world; none of us are. However, that does not mean I am not going to do my part. If I want the world to be better, I need to take action and help make it better. Even if I did my BEST, it would not be enough to make a significant change. It was the realization of just how little I can change the world on my own, that drove me to write this book. I can't do this alone. However, if I can help enough people to do their best, then I believe a change will be noticed. I'm referring to a change in the way people treat each other, how businesses and leaders choose to function with integrity and honor, and changes that make the world better.

I mentioned that my youth pastor called me a world changer as a high schooler. I believed those words. As a student, I wanted to make a difference, but I learned that I would fall short on my own. I began to gather those closest to me, and we declared that we would start something new. Our area of influence was using parkour and sports. When we began forming our team, we named our group New Breed Krew. I apologize for the sad choice to use a K instead of a C in "Crew." We were young. We hoped to be different. We did not use our talents to gain popularity or fame but to help make a difference. We didn't want the attention to be on us but instead chose to give God the glory. We knew it would take time, but we wanted to start helping others see the value of giving credit instead of receiving it. Instead of becoming the best, we wanted to help others be their best. We didn't want to merely fit into the status quo; we wanted to change it. Our goal was to raise the standard.

In life, we should never be okay with average. Instead, we should always be aiming to improve, to go beyond. When I look at the upcoming practitioners of parkour, I am blown away by their creativity and ability to surpass what was expected to be possible when I started. We see this incredible growth in talent due to individuals who refuse to settle for average. Whenever someone comes up with a new style or trick, they strive to surpass it, become better, and aim at a new best. This lifestyle is true in almost every pursuit. We can see this in musicians who keep pushing the boundaries of skill when playing or writing. It is seen in artists who make designs that seem so realistic that you can't tell the difference between real and man-made from an arm's length away. Developers are continually blurring the lines between science fiction and reality. Businesses are finding new strategies to earn financial gain and to capitalize on trends. All of this is happening because of people who are waking up every day thinking, "How can today be better than yesterday?" Or, "What is the best that I can do today?" The question is, are you one of those people?

I hope that you are ready to step outside the boundaries of the status quo. Each day you wake up, you get to decide if you are going to do something good, better, or best. Remember the quote from St. Jerome at the beginning of this book: "Good, better, best. Never let it rest. 'Til your good is better, and your better is best." Another pastor and author, Craig Groeschel, wrote, "Normal people allow good things to become the enemy of the best things." You can do incredible things. Your talents, skills, and experience are just factors in the equation, but in the end, YOU are capable. We can improve talent, learn new skills, and gain more experience, but it is you who chooses how to use these factors to make a difference. I hope that you make the best choices that lead to the best outcomes. I hope that you will always aim to be more than just better. I believe that you can **be best!**

NOTES

Introduction:

1. A quote by Jerome. (n.d.). Retrieved June 21, 2020, from https://www.goodreads.com/quotes/9088059-good-better-best-never-let-it-rest-til-your-good

2. Nelson, J., & Carloni, A. (Directors). (2018). Kung Fu Panda 3 [Motion picture]. Dreamworks.

3. Koike, T. (Director), & Kawajiri, Y. (Writer). (2003, June 3). World Record [Television series episode]. In The Animatrix.

4. Roger Bannister: First sub-four-minute mile. (n.d.). Retrieved June 21, 2020, from https://www.guinnessworldrecords.com/records/hall-of-fame/first-sub-four-minute-mile

5. Ludwing van Beethoven Biography (H. Salter, Trans.). (n.d.). Retrieved June 21, 2020, from http://www.lvbeethoven.com/Bio/BiographyLudwig.html

6. Strickland, S. (2018, December 31). Call Box: Ann Adams became renowned artist despite paralysis. Retrieved June 21, 2020, from https://www.jacksonville.com/news/20181230/call-box-ann-adams-became-renowned-artist-despite-paralysis

7. E, N. (2009, July 8). Best advice I ever got. Retrieved June 21, 2020, from https://money.cnn.com/galleries/2009/fortune/0906/gallery.best_advice_i_ever_got2.fortune/11.html

Chapter One:

1. Proverbs 4:7 (NIV)

2. Regret: Definition of Regret by Oxford Dictionary on Lexico.com also meaning of Regret. (n.d.). Retrieved June 21, 2020, from https://www.lexico.com/en/definition/regret

3. Matthew 7:24-27 (NIV)

4. John D. Rockefeller: The Ultimate Oil Man. (n.d.). Retrieved June 21, 2020, from https://u-s-history.com/pages/h957.html

5. Rosenberg, J. (2017, March 6). A Profile of Henry Ford, Founder of the Ford Motor Company. Retrieved June 21, 2020, from https://www.thoughtco.com/henry-ford-1779249

6. Short Bio: All about Steve Jobs.com. (n.d.). Retrieved June 21, 2020, from https://allaboutstevejobs.com/bio/short_bio

7. Maxwell, J. C. (2008). Leadership Gold: Lessons I've Learned from a Lifetime of Leading. Nashville, TN: HarperCollins Leadership.

8. Christie, M. (Director). (2003). Jump London [Television broadcast]. In Jump London.

Chapter Two:

1. Quote Investigator. (2015, April 18). Whatever You Are, Try To Be a Good One. Retrieved June 21, 2020, from https://quoteinvestigator.com/2014/10/03/be-good/

2.   Merriam-Webster. (n.d.). House. In Merriam-Webster.com dictionary. Retrieved June 21, 2020, from https://www.merriam-webster.com/dictionary/house

3.   Merriam-Webster. (n.d.). Foundation. In Merriam-Webster.com dictionary. Retrieved June 21, 2020, from https://www.merriam-webster.com/dictionary/foundation

4.   Quote from Dr. Seuss. (n.d.). Retrieved June 21, 2020, from http://www.quotationspage.com/quote/29739.html

5.   ESC. (2000, October 24). Re: The apple never falls far from the tree [Web log comment]. Retrieved June 21, 2020, from https://www.phrases.org.uk/bulletin_board/6/messages/445.html

6.   A quote from Harry Potter and the Order of the Phoenix. (n.d.). Retrieved June 21, 2020, from https://www.goodreads.com/quotes/619002-a-good-first-impression-can-work-wonders

7.   Goman, C. (2015, August 25). Seven Seconds to Make a First Impression. Retrieved June 21, 2020, from https://www.forbes.com/sites/carolkinseygoman/2011/02/13/seven-seconds-to-make-a-first-impression/

8.   Belludi, N. (2017, October 27). Albert Mehrabian's 7-38-55 Rule of Personal Communication. Retrieved June 21, 2020, from https://www.rightattitudes.com/2008/10/04/7-38-55-rule-personal-communication/

9.   Picasso, P. (1911). The Accordionist [Digital image]. Retrieved June 21, 2020, from https://www.pablopicasso.org/accordionist.jsp

10. Ephesians 2:10 (NASB)

11. Thayer, J., & Smith. (1999). In The NAS New Testatment Greek Lexicon. Retrieved June 21, 2020, from https://www.biblestudytools.com/lexicons/greek/nas/poiema.html

12. Stevens, K. (2016, July 14). Building a Brain. Retrieved June 21, 2020, from https://www.usnews.com/opinion/articles/2016-07-14/babies-brains-are-shaped-by-interaction-at-earlier-age-than-parents-assume

13. Biography.com Editors. (2019, June 22). Louis Braille Biography. Retrieved June 21, 2020, from https://www.biography.com/scholar/louis-braille

14. Russo, A., & Russo, J. (Directors). (2019). Avengers: Endgame [Motion picture]. Marvel.

Chapter Three:

1.   Our Pizza. (n.d.). Retrieved June 21, 2020, from https://www.papajohns.com/company/how-we-make-better-pizza.html

2.   What Does Hindsight is 20 20 Mean? (n.d.). Retrieved June 21, 2020, from https://writingexplained.org/idiom-dictionary/hindsight-is-20-20

3.   A quote by Helen Keller. (n.d.). Retrieved June 21, 2020, from https://www.goodreads.com/quotes/12998-the-most-pathetic-person-in-the-world-is-some-one

4.   Ambition: Definition of Ambition by Oxford Dictionary on Lexico.com also meaning of Ambition. (n.d.). Retrieved June 21, 2020, from https://www.lexico.com/en/definition/ambition

5.   Biography.com Editors. (2019, October 24). Mark Zuckerberg Biography. Retrieved June 21, 2020, from https://www.biography.com/business-figure/mark-zuckerberg

6.   Fraser Doherty - The Adventures of Jam Boy. (n.d.). Retrieved June 21, 2020, from https://www.fraserdoherty.com/pages/biography

7.   Cunningham, J. M. (2020, April 15). Justin Bieber. Retrieved June 21, 2020, from https://www.britannica.com/biography/Justin-Bieber

8.   Stagliano, K. (n.d.). About Us – Welcome to Katie's Krops ! Retrieved June 21, 2020, from https://katieskrops.com/about-us/

9.   A quote by Zig Ziglar. (n.d.). Retrieved June 21, 2020, from https://www.goodreads.com/quotes/218961-if-you-can-dream-it-then-you-can-achieve-it

10.   Jain, R. (2011, June 12). What is the origin of the phrase "Jack of all trades"? Retrieved June 21, 2020, from https://timesofindia.indiatimes.com/What-is-the-origin-of-the-phrase-Jack-of-all-trades/articleshow/8820631.cms

11.   Kleeman, S. (2016, September 26). Even Google Got Fooled by a Fake Harriet Tubman Quote. Retrieved June 21, 2020, from https://gizmodo.com/even-google-got-fooled-by-a-fake-harriet-tubman-quote-1772260111

12.   Doran, G. T. (1981). There's a S.M.A.R.T. way to write management's goals and objectives. Management Review, Volume 70, Issue 11(AMA FORUM), pp. 35-36.

13.   Boldness: Definition of Boldness by Oxford Dictionary on Lexico.com also meaning of Boldness. (n.d.). Retrieved June 21, 2020, from https://www.lexico.com/en/definition/boldness

14.   Entrepreneur Staff. (2017, May 26). 10 Quotes From John F. Kennedy on Leadership and Personal Growth. Retrieved June 21, 2020, from https://www.entrepreneur.com/article/294906

15.   Tired of Keeping Up with the Joneses? [Web log post]. (n.d.). Retrieved June 21, 2020, from https://www.daveramsey.com/blog/tired-of-keeping-up-with-the-joneses

16.   The Wright Brothers & the Invention of the Aerial Age. (n.d.). Retrieved June 21, 2020, from https://airandspace.si.edu/exhibitions/wright-brothers/online/index.cfm

17.   Kelly, F. C. (n.d.). A Study in Human Incredulity. Retrieved June 21, 2020, from http://www.wright-brothers.org/History_Wing/Aviations_Attic/They_Wouldnt_Believe/They_Wouldnt_Believe_the_Wrights_Had_Flown.htm

18.   Howes, L. (2012, July 19). 20 Lessons from Walt Disney on Entrepreneurship, Innovation and Chasing Your Dreams. Retrieved June 21, 2020, from https://www.forbes.com/sites/lewishowes/2012/07/17/20-business-quotes-and-lessons-from-walt-disney/

19.   Confidence: Definition of Confidence by Oxford Dictionary on Lexico.com also meaning of Confidence. (n.d.). Retrieved June 21, 2020, from https://www.lexico.com/en/definition/confidence

20.   Hebrews 10:35 (NKJV)

21.   Emotional Contagion - IResearchNet. (2016, January 22). Retrieved June 21, 2020, from http://psychology.iresearchnet.com/social-psychology/emotions/emotional-contagion/

22.   Quote of the Month: "Where there is No Vision, There is no Hope" ~ George Washington Carver. (2020, January 31). Retrieved June 21, 2020, from https://kyforagenews.com/2020/01/31/quote-of-the-month-where-there-is-no-vision-there-is-no-hope-george-washington-carver/

Chapter Four:

1. Sinek, S. (2009). Start with Why: How Great Leaders Inspire Everyone to Take Action. London: Portfolio Penguin.

2. Stratford, S. (2019, September 25). Clear Fork football player saves neighbor's life by lifting car. Retrieved June 21, 2020, from https://fox8.com/news/clear-fork-football-player-saves-neighbors-life-by-lifting-car/

3. Romans 12:9-13 (NLT)

4. 2 Corinthians 9:6-7 (NIV)

5. Whitaker, L. (2018, May 03). How does Thinking Positive Thoughts Affect Neuroplasticity? Retrieved June 21, 2020, from https://meteoreducation.com/how-does-thinking-positive-thoughts-affect-neuroplasticity

6. A quote by Zig Ziglar. (n.d.). Retrieved June 21, 2020, from https://www.goodreads.com/quotes/9030465-it-is-your-attitude-not-your-aptitude-that-determines-your

7. Merriam-Webster. (n.d.). Faith. In Merriam-Webster.com dictionary. Retrieved June 20, 2020 from https://www.merriam-webster.com/dictionary/faith

8. Hebrews 11:1 (NASB)

9. Doubt: Definition of Doubt by Oxford Dictionary on Lexico.com also meaning of Doubt. (n.d.). Retrieved June 21, 2020, from https://www.lexico.com/en/definition/doubt

10. Allers, R., & Minkoff, R. (Directors), & Mecchi, I., Roberts, J., Woolverton, L., Rice, T., & John, E. (Writers). (1994). The Lion King [Motion picture]. United States: Walt Disney Pictures.

11. Macdonald, K. (2019, July 24). What does the phrase 'Hakuna matata' actually mean? Retrieved June 21, 2020, from https://www.classicfm.com/discover-music/hakuna-matata-lyrics-meaning-lion-king/

12. Proverbs 12:25 (NLT)

13. Matthew 6:34 (NASB)

14. Philippians 4:6 (NLT)

15. Ball, P. (2011, September 16). In pursuit of neuroscience: Yo-Yo Ma. Retrieved June 21, 2020, from https://www.ft.com/content/af5633c4-de78-11e0-a2c0-00144feabdc0

Chapter Five:

1. Wolfson, R. (2017, October 31). Uncovering The Two Keys To Leadership Legacy. Retrieved June 21, 2020, from https://www.huffpost.com/entry/uncovering-the-two-keys-to-leadership-legacy_b_59f89e89e4b0de896d3f2b7e?guccounter=1

2. Genesis 2:18 (NIV)

3. Medrut, F. (2018, December 06). 16 Most Remarkable Napoleon Bonaparte Quotes. Retrieved June 21, 2020, from https://www.goalcast.com/2018/12/06/napoleon-bonaparte-quotes/

4. Acts 7:22 (NIV)

5. Exodus 18:13-23 (NIV)

6. Mejia, Z. (2018, January 18). The top 25 US companies to work for if you want to be happier. Retrieved June 21, 2020, from https://www.cnbc.com/2018/01/18/the-top-25-us-companies-to-work-for-if-you-want-to-be-happier.html

7. McGregor, J. (2016, August 13). Tim Cook, the interview: Running Apple 'is sort of a lonely job'. Retrieved June 21, 2020, from https://www.washingtonpost.com/sf/business/2016/08/13/tim-cook-the-interview-running-apple-is-sort-of-a-lonely-job/

8. Spencer, L. (2019, June 1). The Greatest Leader Who Ever Lived! Retrieved June 21, 2020, from https://www.alabamagazette.com/story/2019/06/01/soul-searching/the-greatest-leader-who-ever-lived/1678.html

9. Strock, J. M. (2001). Theodore Roosevelt on Leadership: Executive Lessons from the Bully Pulpit. Roseville, CA: Forum.

10. Melancon, R. (2013, November 24). Shoe Me Your Friends and I'll Show You Your Future [Web log post]. Retrieved June 21, 2020, from https://thibodauxpd.wordpress.com/2013/11/24/show-me-your-friends-and-ill-show-you-your-future/

11. Maxwell, J. C. (2005). The 360 Degree Leader: Developing Your Influence from Anywhere in the Organization. Nashville, TN: Nelson Business.

Chapter Six:

1. Lyn, E. (Director), & Petrie, D. (Writer). (2015, April 10). The Ones We Leave Behind [Television series episode]. In Daredevil. Netflix.

2. Numbers 13:27-28 (NIV)

3. Obiora, S. C. (2019, June 5). Small Trouble [Web log post]. Retrieved June 21, 2020, from https://apoetsbrain.com/2019/06/05/small-trouble/

4. James 1:2-4 (NLT)

Chapter Seven:

1. Michelic, A. T. (2018, January 3). "Whenever you do a thing, act as if all the world were watching" - Thomas Jefferson [Web log post]. Retrieved June 21, 2020, from https://commonchap.com/2018/01/03/whenever-you-do-a-thing-act-as-if-all-the-world-were-watching-thomas-jefferson/

2. Ellis, L. (2020, June 19). The Dash Poem. Retrieved June 21, 2020, from https://thedashpoem.com/

3. Matthew 22:37-39 (NIV)

4. Chapman, G.D. (1992). The Five Love Languages: How to Express Heartfelt Commitment to Your Mate. Chicago, IL: Northfield Publishing.

Final Words:

1. Helen Keller Quotes. (n.d.). Retrieved June 21, 2020, from https://www.brainyquote.com/quotes/helen_keller_142101

2. A quote by Jerome. (n.d.). Retrieved June 21, 2020, from https://www.goodreads.com/quotes/9088059-good-better-best-never-let-it-rest-til-your-good

3. Groeschel, C. (2011). Weird: Because Normal Isn't Working. Grand Rapid, MI: Zondervan

ABOUT THE AUTHOR

Stephen M. Law is a pastor at Harborside Christian Church, an author of ministry resources, a certified life coach, and husband to his wife, Rachel. His love for adventure and challenge has led him to hobbies like parkour, martial arts, scuba diving, gaming, and graphic design. With a Bachelor of Science in Church Ministry, Stephen's passion is to see others become world changers! He has spent the last 15+ years pouring into the lives of children, students, and adults. His unique perspective on life has helped thousands of individuals overcome doubts and obtain renewed purpose.

Learn more about Stephen at www.stephenmlaw.com.

ACKNOWLEGMENTS

God: You made me who I am. I'm thankful for the serendipitous life You gave me.

My parents: You led me in a life of faith and trust. Your direction shaped my life.

My youth pastors: You believed in me and taught me the foundations of leadership.

My wife, Rachel: You supported me. You told me what I needed to hear, even if it wasn't always what I wanted to hear. I love you! You're going to be a great mom.

My middle school leaders: You have supported me in so many ways throughout the years! Thank you for believing in me and helping me change the world through the next generation! So many of you have been like family to Rachel and me. You guys are the BEST, and I'm thankful to call you friends!

Joy Weaver: Other than Rachel, you were the first to read through this book, and helped to bring out its best! You, Paul, Luke, and Grace have always been some of my biggest supporters, and I'm blessed to have you all in my life.

My supporters: I would not be my best without the support of so many friends and family members. Thank you for seeing the best in me and my dreams, and for helping me cultivate them into reality!

TWO PENNY PUBLISHING

Tom: You inspire me to be more. Thank you for sharing your wisdom with me.

Sarah: Thanks for always being a smiling face of encouragement.

Jodi: You and your family have always believed in me since the day we met over ten years ago. John was the first person I met at Harborside, and he immediately had my back. I'm happy I've been able to be a part of Josh, Jordan, Jackson, and Josie's lives through these years!

Holly: Thank you for helping me have a clear and precise message. I'm grateful for the opportunity to know your incredible family. You have all brought so much joy to my life!

And to every reader, thank you for taking steps to be best. This world NEEDS people like you who are willing to make a difference. If we haven't met, I hope to meet you or at least hear about how you are changing the world!